Volume I

THIS COUNTRY OF OURS

The Story of the United States

H. E. Marshall's "This Country of Ours"
Annotated, Expanded, and Updated

Donna-Jean A. Breckenridge

An annotated, expanded, and updated version of H. E. Marshall's *This Country of Ours*, New York: George H. Doran Company, 1917.

ISBN: 9798836808709

Book cover design by Kingdom Covers.com.

Cover art: Jasper Francis Cropsey's "Autumn - On the Hudson River 1860." This image is in the public domain.

To Nate—
For always cheering me on
and for talking to me about history.
I guess now you know what happened at Roanoke.

And to Wendi—
For inspiring me
and making sure I got the story right.
The best chapter is the one you got to read.

I miss you both more than words can say.

Acknowledgements

With gratitude to Henrietta Elizabeth Marshall, whose love for the stories of people of other countries in general, and for America in particular, astounds me. She set an example that went far beyond her time.

I'm so grateful to God for Charlotte Mason, whose life and legacy continue to shape mine, in countless, beautiful ways.

To the AmblesideOnline Community, and to the women who read this book and made suggestions and corrections. It's better because of you.

To the AmblesideOnline Advisory—I simply don't have enough words for Lynn Bruce, Karen Glass, Leslie Laurio, Anne White—and Wendi Capehart. You are the incalculable blessings in my life, the gift I cannot believe I've been given. The safe space. The bee-loud glade. Thank you, with my love.

To my parents, Paul and Lois Anderson, who told me their stories from the time I was little, and whose ongoing story of their own enduring love continues to anchor me through every vicissitude of life.

To my children – Bethany (and Nate…), Nathan, Hannah and Jon, and Niko – I love you more than I can ever describe. And to my grandchildren – Shakaila, Driya, Sadiq, and Jack: MomMom loves you infinity. Being your mother, grandmother, and mother-in-law is the answer to years of prayers, and I still marvel at God's magnificent response.

And an added word to Bethany. Thank you for making it possible for me to write, even in the midst of difficult and trying times, and for always encouraging and supporting me. We would never have written our stories as they have unfolded, but I am daily thankful that we can help each other lean on the One who knows the end from the beginning. He remains, always, safe to trust.

And to America, this country of mine. Your story is worth telling and worth telling well. God bless you, land that I love.

Preface

In 1917, British author Henrietta Elizabeth Marshall wrote *This Country of Ours* (published in the United Kingdom as *The Story of the United States*). She dedicated the book to Peggy Stewardson, and "all the other children, big and little, who made my sojourn in the United States a time of happy memories."

Here's what Marshall wrote to Peggy, in the original preface:

Dear Peggy:

Four years have come and gone since first you asked me to write a Story of the United States "lest you should grow up knowing nothing of your own country." I think, however, that you are not yet very grown up, not yet too "proud and great" to read my book. But I hope that you know something already of the history of your own country. For, after all, you know, this is only a play book. It is not a book which you need to knit your brows over, or in which you will find pages of facts, or politics, or long strings of dates. But it is a book, I hope, which when you lay it down will make you say, "I'm glad that I was born an American. I'm glad that I can salute the stars and stripes as my flag."

Yes, the flag is yours. It is in your keeping and in that of every American boy and girl. It is you who in the next generation must keep it flying still over a people free and brave and true, and never in your lives do aught to dim the shining splendour of its silver stars.

Always your friend,
H. E. Marshall

For many years, boys and girls have read *This Country of Ours* and its stories of the Americans. And now for a new generation of curious and wondering readers, something more is provided with this version.

This volume, the first of what will be a series of four, replaces old terms for Native people with correct tribal names, identifies the sources of quotes and other material, updates information where it is pertinent, and adds American spellings.

But the book is still Marshall's story, and the goal remains the same: to encourage those who are Americans – whether you were born here or you came here from another country – to keep the flag flying over a people 'free and brave and true.' May it ever be so.

Your friend,
Donna-Jean A. Breckenridge

Table of Contents

Introduction to This Country of Ours: The Story of the United States Volume 1

"President Kennedy was shot."

The fourth grader announced it matter-of-factly, with a childish sense that he was imparting a big piece of news to the teacher and her classroom, yet without fully understanding the weight of what he had just said. Miss Ward stared in shock at this little boy whose arrival usually meant just his assigned chore of coming in at 2:30 to clean our first-grade classroom's blackboards.

I remember sitting there in the sudden silence, knowing this was a big deal. Even at six years of age, I knew who President Kennedy was. I knew that he had a little girl who was my age and a little boy just a little younger than my brother. I knew his wife was very pretty. My parents, brother, and I had gone on a trip to Washington, D.C., and had even visited the White House. I remember the tour guide saying that the President was not there that day, so I stopped looking for him.

After I walked home from school on that November afternoon, my mother told me what CBS-TV anchorman Walter Cronkite had just announced: the 35th President of the United States had been assassinated.

In my generation, it was a common thing to say that you knew where you were when you heard that news. But it was not just news. It was history.

That's the way history works. At one point, it was news. At one point, it was something brand new that was happening to people just like me. And it was a story to be told.

That was the first big news story that I remember. There would be many more to follow, in what became my lifelong interest in current events. As a young girl, I remember sitting in a special assembly when I was in fifth grade. The principal told all of us there that although we may not have known before that spring day who Martin Luther King, Jr. was, from that point on we would never forget. He was right.

I remember being with my family at a truck stop somewhere on our way to a summer Bible conference where my father would be the preacher for the week. And on a small black and white TV perched above the counter, there was a fuzzy video and the astronaut's words, "That's one small step for man, one giant leap for mankind."

After the first man – an American – set foot on the moon, my mother told me a story about the second man on Apollo 11 with Neil Armstrong. Back when she was in junior high, all her town was talking about Buzz Aldrin, the big star on the Montclair High School football team. And now here he was, leaving an American flag on Tranquility Base. The local boy made good that time, for sure.

I remember a long war that affected my classmates and the people in my church. My violin teacher was drafted suddenly, and since I really disliked the older man that took his place, I quit. I blamed the war on what I told myself would certainly have been a stellar career as a violinist. Far more significant than that, there was a girl in my class whose older brother was serving in Vietnam, and I had a friend at church whose brother was killed on a military training mission overseas. They never found his body. The American flag was draped over the communion table at the funeral service, with his framed picture placed above it.

I remember being on the bus headed for Bloomfield High School each morning and hearing the bits of news on the radio, above the din and in between the rock music, something about a hotel named Watergate, secret tapes, indictments, and special prosecutors, and it all just sounded complicated. And then there was a new president, a pardon, and the fall of Saigon. The new president had a daughter who was also my age, so I wrote her a letter, and she wrote me back. Susan Ford said she had a cat. Her name was Shan. That part I could understand.

There were the stories my parents told my brother and me about growing up, of what life was like on the American home front during World War II. My mother told me how no one could buy nylon stockings anymore because of the war, and how she and her girlfriends once put glue on their legs to make their bobby socks stay put. She told me that she learned current events with her older sister when they went to the theater and watched the newsreels right before the movie started. When she was a young girl, she believed that if the war ever ended, there would be no more newspapers, because she thought there would be no more news.

My father said the noise of celebration was so intense on V-J Day (Victory over Japan), their dog went crazy and had to be put down. A happier memory for him was listening to the *Lone Ranger* and *The Shadow* on the radio, and he told my brother and me all about it, even down to the theme songs and the commercials. I know every word to the intro of "those thrilling days of yesteryear" that followed the William Tell overture, and Chuck and I can still sing the commercial "Shredded Ralstons for your breakfast." My Dad even taught the grandchildren that song. I guess giving you "lots of cowboy energy" was a serious lure for boys and girls back then.

I heard stories from my maternal grandmother about what it was like growing up in a Swedish coal-mining town in western Pennsylvania, where she didn't even learn English until she was five years old, and my paternal grandmother regaled me with her growing up in England's Lake District before coming to America when she was 18. My grandfather's stories had a redemptive power and were often included in his messages from the pulpit – tales of traveling to Japan after World War II to preach, and of years later meeting Mitsuo Fuchida, the bomber aviator who led the raid on Pearl Harbor, and Jacob DeShazer, one of Doolittle's Raiders who later was a P.O.W. in a Japanese prison. Both men, once atheists, became Christians, and they even preached together at times.

I did not have many conversations with my great-grandparents. I just recall that my great-grandmother had a Christmas birthday, made pumpkin pie, loved Jesus, and talked a lot, and that my great-grandfather had worked in a shipyard down in Camden, and that he turned his hearing aid off when his wife talked too much. But it fascinated me that they were born in the 1800s, during another era and another century.

These were all current events at the time, but they are now history. They are now stories that belong in family lore, and some of them belong in history books.

As a little girl, I lived in the small town of Pequannock, New Jersey, which then had a one-room library. I actually recall thinking I would try to read every one of the children's books in it. Needless to say, even in such a tiny library, I did not accomplish that goal. In that library as well as the library in the basement of my grammar school, I sought out books of fiction that would become my favorites. *Heidi* and *A Little Princess* are so ingrained in my childhood mind that I have to remind myself that they are not my actual memories.

I also discovered biographies, especially the *Childhood of Famous Americans* series. Abigail Adams was my favorite. One Halloween, I even dressed up as a colonial lady, long before such a selection might be seen as out of place. I remember the first time I thought it would be interesting to read about boys in history as well, and so I read as many books about American historical figures as I could.

But it wasn't just reading about them that interested me. I would think about history even when I was playing. I can recall standing at the edge of a section of woods or by a field or even in a park. That was a favorite thing to do – to find an area that was completely untouched by anything modern – no road, no sidewalk, no telephone poles, no cars or even neighborhood houses in my sight – and try to imagine what it must have been like to be a young woman in a Leni Lenape Indian tribe, or someone like Molly Pitcher, helping the men on the Revolutionary War battlefield, or an enslaved girl finding her way to the next stop on the Underground Railroad. I thought a lot about what life was like for people who lived long ago.

Whenever I got to visit different historical sites, I would do the same thing. I would try to look at one part of the view of the Potomac from the porch at Mount Vernon, or stand in a corner of the old Capitol building in Williamsburg, or sit on the field on a hot day in Gettysburg, and I would think about what it was like – because at one point, it was the present. It was news. At one moment in time, it was happening right then, to someone just like me.

A month after the life-changing event of becoming a mother in January 1986, I found the writing of Charlotte Mason, a British educator at the turn of the twentieth century. I read Susan Schaeffer Macaulay's *For the Children's Sake*, and a few years later, I read the newly reprinted editions of Charlotte Mason's six-volume series on education. This broadened my thinking and gave me a philosophy that fit so many of the ideas I had grown up with and had come to value.

So when my daughter reached school age, my husband and I made the decision to homeschool her, using that philosophy. In 1990, things were not as fleshed out as they are now for a CM education, and I was on my own in finding my way. Choosing the books was not a simple matter, to start with. They had to be good. They had to be the highest literary quality. In this, Charlotte Mason herself understood my plight. She wrote, "It is not at all easy to choose the right history books for children. Mere summaries of fact must, as we have seen, be eschewed; and we must be equally careful to avoid generalisations." (*Home Education*, Volume 1, p. 287)

A lot of history books for children today are flashy. They have an overabundance of pictures or sidebars or questions jumping out in a cartoon speech balloon. The layout assumes a reader who is already uninterested, so the author works hard to make the content more intriguing. But history is more than a collection of dates and dead people, with lots of war and long-gone customs and practices. History is "an entrancing subject of study," Mason wrote, and when it is "written in good and simple English and with a certain charm of style, (the books will) lend themselves admirably to narration." (*Home Education*, Volume 1, pp. 291, 289).

Narration, as Karen Glass writes in her seminal book on the topic, is "the art of telling." (*Know and Tell, The Art of Narration*, 2018, p. 1) It is the child's telling-back, in his or her own words, what he or she has read or has heard in a read-aloud. Narration can be oral or written, and it is a foundational element of a Charlotte Mason education, as it develops the habit of attention, it is the essence of writing and of thinking well, and it is the connective tissue that builds relationships, making knowledge a part of the reader. In short, it is the route to "become partakers in that universal quest for wisdom that has been going on for as long as people have been thinking and speaking, and which will not end while the world lasts." (*Know and Tell*, p. 12)

Eventually as my family grew (we would add a son, another daughter, and many years later, another son), so did the brand-new world of the internet. In the mid to late 1990s, I met other women online who were also interested in researching and creating an education based on Charlotte Mason's educational principles: that the mind feeds on ideas, that education was an atmosphere, a discipline, and a life, that children are born persons, and that education is the science of relations. It was exciting to get to know other women who were incorporating all of this into their homeschools as well.

We shared ideas, and we shared resources. We encouraged one another, prayed for one another, wrote about good days and bad days, and dreamed together of how to spread this life-giving education to even more children. We did all this on an e-mail list. For the most part, none of us had met one another yet in real life.

My oldest daughter was at this point in junior high, approaching high school. While other women had done what I had done – put together an elementary school education based on these principles – there were very few who were attempting to shape a Charlotte Mason-styled curriculum plan for high school. So I decided to design one myself. And about that same time, a group of women from our large online group began to think through what a Charlotte Mason education would look like if it were as close as possible to what she had done.

A few from that smaller group became known as the Advisory, and then (partly because of my work on a high school plan), I was invited to join them. We worked day and night, it seemed, on what would eventually become a complete 12-year online curriculum, totally and permanently free for anyone who wishes to use it. And those Advisory members – Lynn Bruce, Wendi Capehart, Karen Glass, Leslie Laurio, and Anne White - became and remain my closest friends. The official launch for what we called "AmblesideOnline" was Independence Day, July 4, 2001. We have continued to work together daily on what we call "AO" ever since.

In those early years we were choosing history books for AmblesideOnline. In *Toward a Philosophy of Education*, Mason's sixth volume in the series, she referred to *Our Island Story*. It was published in 1905 in England, and later abroad as *An Island Story*, and it had as its subtitle, *A Child's History of England*. It was written by H. E. Marshall, a British woman who wrote histories of different countries for children.

The women who were pioneering this education were incredible at finding vintage books, and one of them found a companion volume by Marshall, called *This Country of Ours*. It was published in America 1917, and two years later, it was published in the UK under the title *The Story of the United States*.

The Advisory members were not alone in doing the work of putting out-of-print, public domain books online. We had a vast community of women around the world who wanted to participate. So anyone who found a rare copy of one of these books would take pictures of the pages, then e-mail the images to the women who had volunteered to type them up. *This Country of Ours* has over six hundred pages, and when they were all transcribed and collected, Leslie contacted an online book site called Celebration of Women Writers to see if they might be interested in housing the file on their site. They agreed, and we linked the formerly obscure *This Country of Ours* to our AmblesideOnline website and made it accessible to anyone, anywhere.

As we have stated on AmblesideOnline, "*This Country of Ours* is a classic work for which we have found no equal, and it is an important spine in the AO curriculum." Marshall writes with a respect for children, in literary language, as a champion of people's rights, and with an understanding of the child's need for stories of courage.

But 1917 is a long time ago. I like to think that if Marshall were alive today, she would update *This Country of Ours*. It contains terms in it that were in common usage in her day but are no longer considered acceptable. There are quotation marks around passages without any citation or indication of where they came from. There are English spellings of words (in a book about American history), and there are some stories that are incomplete, or that could use another sentence or another paragraph to give it more context. There are spots where the addition of a comma would make read-aloud easier. But even with these adjustments, the story itself is powerful and true and worthy of reading.

Thanks to a suggestion from Karen, this is the first of what will be four books: the current *This Country of Ours* will be divided up into three volumes, and the fourth will be my original book on the century that follows the ending of H. E. Marshall's book. In this volume, I have done several things that I hope will enhance the use of *This Country of Ours* for a new generation.

I have updated words to be more in line with American spelling. I have replaced words in the narrative that have lost their primary meaning. I have replaced generic or outdated terms with the correct tribal names of Native people.

I have also added notes at the end of each chapter. I put them there rather than at the bottom of the page or at the end of the book to maintain a seamless read yet provide for accessibility. I have checked each of Marshall's quotes, and where possible, I have listed their source. I have added definitions to certain words, as well as pronunciation guides for names and tribes. And where warranted, I have added further explanations or information about other aspects of these historical events.

This volume covers the time from the Vikings, where Marshall begins the account, up to the early 1600s. Indigenous people are a significant part of this story, and a note found in chapter one bears repeating here, so that it is not missed.

My research brought me to this conclusion for this book series:

Note regarding terminology:

"What is the correct terminology: American Indian, Indian, Native American, or Native? All of the above terms are acceptable. The consensus, however, is that whenever possible, Native people prefer to be called by their specific tribal name. Native peoples in the Western Hemisphere are best understood as thousands of distinct communities and cultures. Many Native communities have distinct languages, religious beliefs, ceremonies, and social and political systems. The inclusive word 'Indian' (a name, used by the Spanish to refer to much of southern Asia, given by Christopher Columbus who mistakenly believed he had sailed to India) says little about the diversity and independence of the cultures." ("Do All Indians Live in Tipis? Questions and Answers from the National Museum of the American Indian," Smithsonian Institution, 2019, p.132.)

In each instance in this volume, I have sought to use the correct tribal name, but where I could not be certain, I have opted to use the terms "Indian" or "Native people."

And this note is important at the outset as well:

Note regarding the use of the word 'discovery':

In some instances, I have changed that word in these chapters to reflect the fact that people already lived in so-called 'discovered' places. However, the word still has meaning in English usage in that one can discover something that is new to that person (or to the people that person represents), without being the very first to find it. In that sense, the word 'discovery' is kept where appropriate.

Even with the changes in this book and in subsequent volumes, this is still the "Story of the United States." It is the story of people brought together not because they are of the same race or ethnicity or background or even with a common journey here, but because they share belief in a core of ideas. Some of those ideas had to be forged in a fire before they were available to all, but they were American ideas still, and they were worthy of the struggle and worthy of the fight, to provide and protect that freedom for every American.

Charlotte Mason wrote, "Next in order to religious knowledge, history is the pivot upon which our curriculum turns." (Volume 6, p. 273) And now is the time. "It is never too late to mend but we may not delay to offer such a liberal and generous diet of History to every child in the country as to give weight to his decisions, consideration to his actions and stability to his conduct; that stability, the lack of which has plunged us into many a stormy sea of unrest." (p. 179)

In our stormy sea of unrest, let's begin anew to look at *This Country of Ours—The Story of the United States*.

Chapter 1

How the Vikings of Old Sought and Found New Lands

In days long, long ago, there dwelt in Greenland a king named Eric the Red. He was a man mighty in war, and men held him in high honor.

Now one day to the court of Eric there came Bjarni, the son of Heriulf. This Bjarni was a far traveler. He had sailed many times upon the seas, and when he came home, he had ever some fresh tale of marvel and adventure to tell. But this time he had a tale to tell more marvelous than any before. For he told how far away across the sea of Greenland, where no Viking had sailed before, he had found a new, strange land.

But when the people asked news of this unknown land, Bjarni could tell them little, for he had not set foot upon those far shores. Therefore, the people scorned him.

"Truly you have little hardihood," they said, "else you had gone ashore, and seen for yourself, and had given us good account of this land."

But although Bjarni could tell nought of the new strange land, save that he had seen it, the people thought much about it, and there was great talk about voyages and discoveries, and many longed to sail forth and find again the land which Bjarni the Traveler had seen. But more than any other in that kingdom, Leif, the son of Eric the Red, longed to find that land. So Leif went to Eric and said:

"Oh my father, I fain would seek the land which Bjarni the Traveler has seen. Give me gold that I may buy his ship and sail away upon the seas to find it."

Then Eric the Red gave his son gold in great plenty. "Go, my son," he said. "Buy the ship of Bjarni the Traveler, and sail to the land of which he tells."

Then Leif, quickly taking the gold, went to Bjarni and bought his ship.

Leif was a tall man, of great strength and noble bearing. He was also a man of wisdom, and just in all things, so that men loved and were ready to obey him.

Now, therefore, many men came to him offering to be his companions in adventure, until soon they were a company of thirty-five men. They were all men tall and of great strength, with fair golden hair and eyes blue as the sea upon which they loved to sail, save only Tyrker the German.

Long time this German had lived with Eric the Red and was much beloved by him. Tyrker also loved Leif dearly, for he had known him since he was a child and was indeed his foster father. So he was eager to go with Leif upon this adventurous voyage. Tyrker was very little and plain. His forehead was high and his eyes small and restless. He wore shabby clothes, and to the blue-eyed, fair-haired giants of the North, he seemed indeed a sorry-looking fellow. But all that mattered little, for he was a clever craftsman, and Leif and his companions were glad to have him go with them.

Then, all things being ready, Leif went to his father and, bending his knee to him, prayed him to be their leader.

But Eric the Red shook his head. "Nay, my son," he said. "I am old and stricken in years, and no more able to endure the hardships of the sea."

"Yet come, my father," pleaded Leif, "for of a certainty if you do, good luck will go with us."

Then Eric looked longingly at the sea. His heart bade him go out upon it once again ere he died. So he yielded to the prayers of his son and, mounting upon his horse, he rode towards the ship.

When the seafarers saw him come, they set up a shout of welcome. But when Eric was not far from the ship, the horse upon which he was riding stumbled, and he was thrown to the ground. He tried to rise but could not, for his foot was sorely wounded.

Seeing that, he cried out sadly, "It is not for me to discover new lands. Go ye without me."

So Eric the Red returned to his home, and Leif went on his way to his ship with his companions.

Now they busied themselves and set their dragon-headed vessel in order. And when all was ready, they spread their brightly-colored sails and set out into the unknown sea.

Westward and ever westward they sailed towards the setting of the sun. For many days they sailed, yet they saw no land: nought was about them but the restless, tossing waves. But at length one day to their watching eyes, there appeared a faint gray line far on the horizon. Then their hearts bounded for joy. They had not sailed in vain, for land was near.

"Surely," said Leif, as they drew close to it, "this is the land which Bjarni saw. Let it not be said of us that we passed it by as he did."

So, casting anchor, Leif and his companions launched a boat and went ashore. But it was no fair land to which they had come. Far inland, great snow-covered mountains rose, and between them and the sea lay flat and barren rock, where no grass or green thing grew. It seemed to Leif and his companions that there was no good thing in this land.

"I will call it Helluland or Stone Land," said Leif.

Then he and his companions went back to the ship and put out to sea once more. They came to land again after some time, and again they cast anchor and launched a boat and went ashore. This land was flat. Broad stretches of white sand sloped gently to the sea, and behind the level plain was thickly wooded.

"This land," said Leif, "shall also have a name after its nature." So he called it Markland or Woodland.

Then again Leif and his companions returned to the ship, and mounting into it, they sailed away upon the sea. And now fierce winds arose, and the ship was driven before the blast so that for days these seafarers thought no more of finding new lands, but only of the safety of their ship.

But at length the wind fell, and the sun shone forth once more. Then again they saw land, and launching their boat, they rowed ashore.

To the eyes of these seafaring men, who for many days had seen only the wild waste of waters, the land seemed passing fair. For the grass was green, and as the sun shone upon it, it seemed to sparkle with a thousand diamonds. When the men put their hands upon the grass and touched their mouths with their hands and drank the dew, it seemed to them that never before had they tasted anything so sweet. So pleasant the land seemed to Leif and his companions that they determined to pass the winter there. They therefore drew their ship up the river which flowed into the sea and cast anchor.

Then they carried their hammocks ashore and set to work to build a house.

When the house was finished, Leif called his companions together and spoke to them.

"I will now divide our company into two bands," he said, "so that we may explore the country round about. One half shall stay at home, and the other half shall explore the land. But they who go to explore must not go so far away that they cannot return home at night, nor must they separate from each other, lest they be lost."

And as Leif said, so it was done. Each day a company set out to explore, and sometimes Leif went with the exploring party, and sometimes he stayed at home. But each day as evening came, they all returned to their house and told what they had seen.

At length, however, one day, when those who had gone abroad returned, one of their number was missing, and when the roll was called, it was found that it was Tyrker the German who had strayed. Thereat Leif was sorely troubled, for he loved his foster father dearly. So he spoke sternly to his men, reproaching them for their careless-ness in letting Tyrker separate from them, and taking twelve of his men with him, he set out at once to search for his foster father. But they had not gone far when, to their great joy, they saw their lost comrade coming towards them.

"Why art thou so late, oh my foster father?" cried Leif, as he ran to him. "Why hast thou gone astray from the others?"

But Tyrker paid little heed to Leif's questions. He was strangely excited, and rolling his eyes wildly, he laughed and spoke in German, which no one understood. At length, however, he grew calmer and spoke to them in their own language. "I did not go much farther than the others," he said. "But I have found something new. I have found vines and grapes."

"Is that indeed true, my foster father?" said Leif.

"Of a certainty it is true," replied Tyrker. "For I was born where vines grow freely."

This was great news, and all the men were eager to go and see for themselves the vines which Tyrker had discovered. But it was already late, so they all returned to the house and waited with what patience they could until morning.

Then, as soon as it was day, Tyrker led his companions to the place where he had found the grapes. And when Leif saw them, he called the land Vineland because of them. He also decided to load his ship with grapes and wood and depart homeward. So each day the men gathered grapes and felled trees, until the ship was full. Then they set sail for home.

The winds were fair, and with but few adventures they arrived safely at home. There they were received with great rejoicing. Henceforth Leif was called Leif the Lucky, and he lived ever after in great honor and plenty, and the land which he had discovered, men called Vineland the Good.

In due time, however, Eric the Red died, and after that Leif the Lucky sailed no more upon the seas, for his father's kingdom was now his, and he must needs stay at home to rule his land. But Leif's brother Thorvald greatly desired to go to Vineland so that he might explore the country still further.

Then when Leif saw his brother's desire, he said to him, "If it be thy will, brother, thou mayest go to Vineland in my ship."

At that Thorvald rejoiced greatly, and gathering thirty men he set sail, crossed the sea without adventure, and came to the place where Leif had built his house.

There he and his company remained during the winter. Then in the spring, they set forth to explore the coast. After some time, they came upon a fair country where there were many trees.

When Thorvald saw it, he said, "It is so fair a country that I should like to make my home here."

Until this time the Norsemen had seen no inhabitants of the land. But now as they returned to their ship, they saw three mounds upon the shore. When the Norsemen came near, they saw that these three mounds were three canoes, and under each were three men from the Thule tribe armed with bows and arrows, lying in wait. When the Norsemen saw them, they divided their company and put themselves in battle array. And after a fierce battle, they slew the Thules, save one who fled to his canoe and so escaped.

When the fight was over, the Norsemen climbed upon a high headland and looked round to see if there were signs of any more fighters. Below them they saw several mounds which they took to be the houses of the Thules, and they knew that it behooved them therefore to be on their guard. But they were too weary to go further and casting themselves down upon the ground where they were, they fell into a heavy sleep.

Suddenly they were awakened by a great shout, and they seemed to hear a voice cry aloud, "Awake, Thorvald, thou and all thy company, if ye would save your lives. Flee to thy ship with all thy men, and sail with speed from this land."

So Thorvald and his companions fled speedily to their ship, and set it in fighting array. Soon a large crowd of Thule warriors, uttering fearful yells, rushed upon them. The Thule men cast their arrows at the Norsemen, and they fought fiercely for some time. But seeing that their arrows availed little against the strangers, and that on the other hand many of their fellow men were slain, they at last fled.

Then, their enemy being fled, Thorvald, turning to his men, asked, "Are any of you wounded?"

"Nay," they answered. "We are all whole."

"That is well," said Thorvald. "As for me, I am wounded in the armpit by an arrow. Here is the shaft. Of a surety it will cause my death. And now I counsel you, turn homeward with all speed. But carry me first to that headland, which seemed to me to promise so pleasant a dwelling place, and lay me there. Thus it shall be seen that I spoke truth when I wished to abide there. And ye shall place a cross at my feet, and another at my head, and call it Cross Ness ever after."

So Thorvald died. Then his companions buried him as he had bidden them in the land which had seemed to him so fair. And as he had commanded, they set a cross at his feet and another at his head and called the place Cross Ness. Thus the first Norseman was laid to rest in Vineland the Good.

Then when spring came, the Norsemen sailed home to Greenland. And there they told Leif of all the things they had seen and done, and how his brave brother had met his death.

Now when Leif's brother Thorstein heard how Thorvald had died, he longed to sail to Vineland to bring home his brother's body. So once again Leif's ship was made ready, and with five and twenty tall, strong men, Thorstein set forth, taking with him his wife Gudrid.

But Thorstein never saw Vineland the Good. For storms beset his ship, and after being driven hither and thither for many months, he lost all reckoning, and at last came to land in Greenland once more. And there Thorstein died, and Gudrid went home to Leif.

Now there came to Greenland that summer a man of great wealth named Thorfinn. And when he saw Gudrid, he loved her and sought her in marriage, and Leif giving his consent to it, Thorfinn and Gudrid were married.

At this time many people still talked of the voyages to Vineland, and they urged Thorfinn to journey thither and seek to find out more about these strange lands. And more than all the others, Gudrid urged him to go. So at length Thorfinn determined to undertake the voyage. But it came to his mind that he would not merely go to Vineland and return home again. He resolved rather to settle there and make it his home.

Thorfinn, therefore, gathered about sixty men, and those who had wives took also their wives with them, together with their cattle and their household goods.

Then Thorfinn asked Leif to give him the house which he had built in Vineland. And Leif replied, "I will lend the house to you, but I will not give it."

So Thorfinn and Gudrid and all their company sailed out to sea, and without adventures arrived safely at Leif's house in Vineland.

There they lived all that winter in great comfort. There was no lack of food either for man or beast, and the cattle they had brought with them roamed at will and fed upon the wide prairie lands.

All winter and spring the Norsemen dwelt in Vineland, and they saw no human beings save themselves. Then one day in early summer they saw a group of Thule people come out of the wood. They were short in height, with great eyes and broad cheeks. The cattle were near, and as these men appeared, the bull began to bellow. And when the Thule heard that sound, they were afraid and fled. For three whole weeks, nothing more was seen of them. After that time, however, the men took courage again and returned. As they approached, they made signs to show that they came in peace, and with them they brought huge bales of furs which they wished to barter.

The Norsemen, it is true, could not understand the language of the Thule, nor could the Thule understand the Norsemen; but by signs they made known that they wished to barter their furs for weapons. This, however, Thorfinn forbade. Instead, he gave them strips of red cloth which they took very eagerly and bound about their heads. Thorfinn also commanded his men to take milk to the Thule, and when they saw it, they were eager to buy and drink it. So that it was said many of them carried away their merchandise in their stomachs.

Thus the days and months passed. Then one summer day, a little son was born to Thorfinn and Gudrid. They called him Snorri, and he was the first child of Europeans to be born on the Continent which later men called the New World. Thus three years went past. But the days were not all peaceful. For quarrels arose between the newcomers and the Thule, and the attacks and revenge led to much killing.

Then Thorfinn said he would no longer stay in Vineland but would return to Greenland. So he and all his company made ready their ship, and sailed out upon the seas, and came at length safely to Greenland.

Then after a time, Thorfinn sailed to Iceland. There he made his home for the rest of his life, the people holding him in high honor. Gudrid, too, was much respected. Snorri, their son who had been born in Vineland, grew to be a man of great renown, a farmer, and a church-builder.

Such are some of the old Norse stories of their first finding of America. The country which Leif called Helluland was most likely Labrador, Markland Newfoundland, and Vineland Nova Scotia.

Besides these, there were many other tales of voyages to Vineland. For after Leif and his brothers, many other Vikings of the North sailed, both from Greenland and from Norway, to the fair western lands. Yet although they sailed there so often, these old Norsemen had no idea that they had reached a vast continent. They thought that Vineland was merely an island, and so the discovery of it made no stir in Europe. By degrees, too, the voyages thither ceased. In days of wild warfare at home, the Norsemen forgot the fair western land which Leif had reached. They heard of it only in minstrel tales, and it came to be for them a sort of fairy land which had no existence, save in a poet's dream.

But now wise men have read these tales with care, and many have come to believe that they are not mere fairy stories. They have come to believe that hundreds of years before Columbus lived, the Vikings of the North sailed the western seas and found the land which lay beyond, the land which we now call America.

Notes:

The material in this chapter can be found in The Saga of the Greenlanders, *one of the Icelandic sagas, written sometime in the 13th century.*

The Thule people were ancestors of today's Inuit. They traveled from Siberia across the Canadian Arctic and spread into northern Greenland.

Note regarding terminology:

*"What is the correct terminology: American Indian, Indian, Native American, or Native? All of the above terms are acceptable. The consensus, however, is that whenever possible, Native people prefer to be called by their specific tribal name. Native peoples in the Western Hemisphere are best understood as thousands of distinct communities and cultures. Many Native communities have distinct languages, religious beliefs, ceremonies, and social and political systems. The inclusive word 'Indian' (a name, used by the Spanish to refer to much of southern Asia, given by Christopher Columbus who mistakenly believed he had sailed to India) says little about the diversity and independence of the cultures." (*Do All Indians Live in Tipis? Questions and Answers from the National Museum of the American Indian, *Smithsonian Institution, 2019, p.132.)*

In each instance in this volume, I have sought to use the correct tribal name, but where I could not be certain, I have opted to use the terms "Indian" or "Native people."

Note regarding the use of the word 'discovery':

In some instances, I have changed that word in these chapters to reflect the fact that people already lived in so-called 'discovered' places. However, the word still has meaning in English usage in that one can discover something that is new to that person (or to the people that person represents), without being the very first to find it. In that sense, the word 'discovery' is kept where appropriate.

More about Thorfinn, Gudrid, and Snorri, and the archeological discoveries that pertain to them can be read here:

https://www.theage.com.au/world/archaeology-team-unlocks-the-saga-of-snorri-thorfinnsson-20020917-gduliy.html

and

http://www.glaumbaer.is/is/information/glaumbaer-farm/the-first-farmer

---

Pronunciation Guide:

Bjarni - BYARN-ee

Heriulf - HARE-ee-ulf

Leif - LAFE

Tyrker - TURE-ker

Helluland - HELL-you-land

Thorvald - TOR-valt

Thule - TOO-lee

Thorstein - TOR-stine

Gudrid - GOOD-rid

Thorfinn - TOR-fin

Snorri - SNOR-ee

Chapter 2

The Sea of Darkness and the Great Faith of Columbus

In those far-off times, besides the Vikings of the North other daring sailors sailed the seas. But all their sailings took them eastward. For it was from the east that all the trade and the riches came in those days. To India and to far Cathay sailed the merchant through the Red Sea and the Indian Ocean, to return with a rich and fragrant cargo of silks and spices, pearls and priceless gems.

None thought of sailing westward. For to people of those days, the Atlantic Ocean was known as the Outer Sea or the Sea of Darkness. There was nothing to be gained by venturing upon it, much to be dreaded. It was said that huge and horrible sea-dragons lived there, ready to wreck and swallow down any vessel that might venture near. An enormous bird also hovered in the skies, waiting to pounce upon vessels and bear them away to some unknown eyrie. Even if any fool-hardy adventurers should defy these dangers and escape the horror of the dragons and the bird, other perils threatened them. For far in the west there lay a bottomless pit of seething fire.

That was easy of proof. Did not the face of the setting sun glow with the reflected light as it sank in the west? There would be no hope, nor rescue, for any ship that should be drawn into that awful pit.

Also it was believed that the ocean flowed downhill, and that if a ship sailed down too far it would never be able to get back again. These and many other dangers, said the ignorant folk of those days, threatened the rash sailors who should attempt to sail upon the Sea of

Darkness. So it was not wonderful that for hundreds of years men contented themselves with the well-known routes which indeed offered adventure enough to satisfy the heart of the most daring.

But as time passed, these old trade-routes fell more and more into the hands of corsairs. Port after port came under their rule, and these pirates swarmed in the Indian Ocean and Mediterranean, until no European vessel was safe. At every step, European traders found themselves hampered and hindered, in danger of capture and slavery, and they began to long for another way to the lands of spice and pearls.

Then it was that men turned their thoughts to the dread Sea of Darkness. The less ignorant among them had begun to disbelieve the tales of dragons and fiery pits. The world was round, said wise men. Why then, if that were so, India could be reached by sailing west as well as by sailing east.

Many men now came to this conclusion, among them an Italian sailor named Christopher Columbus. The more Columbus thought about his plan of sailing west to reach India, the more he believed in it, and the more he longed to set out. But without a great deal of money, such an expedition was impossible, and Columbus was poor. His only hope was to win the help and friendship of a king, or some other great and wealthy person.

The Portuguese were in those days a seafaring people, and their ships were to be found wherever ships dared go. Indeed, Prince Henry of Portugal did so much to encourage voyages of discovery that he was called Henry the Navigator. And although he was by this time dead, the people still took great interest in voyages of discovery. So at length Columbus determined to go to King John of Portugal to tell him of his plans and ask for his aid.

King John listened kindly enough, it seemed, to what Columbus had to say. But before giving him any answer, he said that he must consult his wise men. These wise men looked upon the whole idea of sailing to the west to reach the east as absurd. So King John refused to give Columbus any help.

Yet although most of King John's wise men thought little of the plan, King John himself thought that there was something in it. But instead of helping Columbus, he meanly resolved to send out an expedition of his own. This he did, and when Columbus heard of it he was so angry that he left Portugal, which for more than ten years he had made his home. He was poor and in debt, so he left the country secretly, in fear of the King, and of those to whom he owed money.

When Columbus thus fled from Portugal, penniless and in debt, he was a man over forty. He was a bitterly disappointed man, too, but he still clung to his great idea. So he sent his brother Bartholomew to England to beg King Henry VII to help him, while he himself turned towards Spain. Bartholomew, however, reached England in an evil hour for his quest. For Henry VII had but newly wrested the crown from Richard III, and so had no thought to spare for unknown lands. Christopher also arrived in Spain at an unfortunate time. For the Spaniards were carrying on a fierce warfare against the Moors, and King Ferdinand and Queen Isabella had little thought or money to spare for any other undertaking. Therefore, although Ferdinand listened to what Columbus had to say, for the time being he could promise no help.

So years passed. Columbus remained in Spain. For in spite of all his rebuffs and disappointments, he did not despair. As the court moved from place to place he followed it, hoping always that the day would come when the King and Queen would listen to him and believe in his great enterprise.

Meanwhile, he lived in want and misery and just kept himself from starvation by making and selling maps. To the common people he seemed a madman, and as he passed through the streets in his worn and threadbare garments, children jeered and pointed fingers of scorn at him.

Yet in spite of mockery and derision, Columbus clung to his belief. Indeed it burned in him so strongly that at length he made others share it too, and men who were powerful at court became his friends.

At last, the war with the Moors ended victoriously for Spain. Then these friends persuaded Queen Isabella to listen again to what

Columbus had to say. To this the Queen consented, and when she heard how poor Columbus was, she sent him some money so that he might buy clothes fit to appear at court.

When Columbus heard the good news, he was overjoyed. As quickly as might be he bought new clothes, and mounting upon a mule, he rode towards Granada. But when Columbus arrived, he found the court still in the midst of rejoicings to celebrate victory. Among the light-hearted, brightly dressed throng, there was no one who had a thought to spare for the melancholy, white-haired dreamer who passed like a dark shadow amidst them. With his fate, as it were, trembling in the balance, Columbus had no heart for rejoicing. So he looked on "with indifference, almost with contempt."

But at length his day came. All the jubilation was over, and Ferdinand and Isabella turned their thoughts to Columbus. He came before them and talked so earnestly of his great project that they could not but believe in it. The day was won. Both King and Queen, but more especially the Queen, were willing to help the great enter-prise. Now, however, Columbus himself all but wrecked his chances. He had dreamed so long about this splendid adventure, he was so filled with belief in its grandeur, that he demanded conditions such as would hardly have been granted to the greatest prince in the land.

Columbus demanded that he should be made admiral and viceroy of all the lands he might discover, and that after his death this honor should descend to his son and to his son's son for ever and ever. He also demanded a tenth part of all the pearls, precious stones, gold, silver and spices, or whatever else he might gain by trade or barter.

At these demands, the grandees of Spain stood aghast. What! This shabby dreamer, this penniless beggar, aspired to honor and dignities fit for a prince! It was absurd, and not to be thought of. If this beggarly sailor would have Spain assist him, he must needs be more humble in suit.

But not one jot would Columbus abate of his demands. So the Council broke up, and Columbus, with anger and disappointment in his heart, mounted his mule and turned his face towards the Court of France. All the seven long years during which he had waited and hoped and prayed in Spain had been wasted. Now he would go to the King of France and make his last appeal there.

But Columbus had left friends behind him, friends who had begun to picture to themselves almost as vividly as he the splendors of the conquest he was to make. Now these friends sought out the Queen. In glowing words, they painted to her the glory and the honor which would come to Spain if Columbus succeeded. And if he failed, why, what were a few thousand crowns, they asked. And as the Queen listened, her heart beat fast; the magnificence of the enterprise took hold upon her, and she resolved that, come what might, Columbus should go forth on his adventure.

Ferdinand, however, still looked coldly on. The war against the Moors had been long and bitter, his treasury was empty. Whence, he asked himself, was money forthcoming for this mad scheme? Isabella, however, had done with prudence and caution. "I undertake the enterprise for my own crown of Castile," she said, "and will pledge my jewels to raise the necessary funds."

While these things were happening Columbus, sick at heart, was slowly plodding on the road to France. But he only went a little way on his long journey. For just as he was entering a narrow pass not far from Granada, where the mountains towered above him, he heard the thud of horses' hoofs.

It was a lonely and silent spot among the hills, where robbers lurked, and where many a man had been slain for the money and jewels he carried. Columbus, however, had nothing to dread: he carried with him neither gold nor jewels. He went forth from Spain a beggar, even as he had come. But if fear he had any, it was soon turned to incredulous joy. For when the horsemen came up, they told Columbus that his friends had won the day for him, and that he must return.

At first Columbus hesitated, for he found it very hard to believe. When, however, the messenger told him that the Queen herself bade him return, he hesitated no longer. Joyfully turning his mule, he hastened back to Granada.

At last Columbus had won his heart's desire, and he had only to gather ships and men and set forth westward. But now a new difficulty arose. For it was out upon the terrible Sea of Darkness that Columbus wished to sail, and men feared to face its terrors.

Week after week went past and not a ship or a man could Columbus get. He persuaded and implored in vain: no man was brave enough to follow him to the unknown horrors of the Sea of Darkness. Therefore as entreaty and persuasion proved of no avail, Columbus sought help from the King, who gave him power to force men to go with him.

Even then, all sorts of difficulties were thrown in the way. Columbus, however, overcame them all, and at length his three ships were ready. But it had taken many months. It was February when he turned back so gladly to Granada; it was the third of August before everything was in order.

Before dawn upon the day he sailed, Columbus entered the church, in the little sea-faring town of Palos where his ships lay at anchor. There he humbly confessed his sins, received the Sacrament, and committed himself to God's all-powerful guidance. The crew, many of them wild, rough fellows, followed his example. Then Columbus stepped on board his ship, the *Santa Maria*, and turned his face westward.

He was filled with exaltation. But all Palos was filled with gloom, and upon the shore a great crowd gathered to bid a last farewell to these daring adventurers. And as the ships spread their sails and sped forth in the morning light, the people wept and lamented sorely, for they never thought again to see their loved ones, who were about to adventure forth upon the terrible Sea of Darkness.

Notes:

Cathay is an old European name for China.

Corsairs: towards the end of the fifteenth century, Muslim privateers began to sail throughout the Mediterranean Sea. They seized European merchant ships to take their cargo and to capture their crew as slaves. Since some came from an area called the Barbary Coast along North Africa, they were also called Barbary pirates. This piracy continued into the nineteenth century.

"Moors" was a term used in reference to the Muslim inhabitants of the Iberian peninsula. The ten-year war between the "Catholic Monarchs"

(Ferdinand and Isabella) and Muhammed XII of Granada (King Boabdil) ended on January 2, 1492, with Boabdil's surrender.

"With indifference, almost with contempt" and "I undertake the enterprise" quotes are from The Life and Voyages of Christopher Columbus, *by Washington Irving, 1828.*

Chapter 3

How Columbus Fared Forth Upon the Sea of Darkness and Came to Pleasant Lands Beyond

At first the voyage upon which Columbus and his daring companions now set forth lay through seas already known, but soon the last landmark was left behind, and the three little vessels, smaller than river craft of today, were alone upon the trackless waste of waters. And when the men saw the last trace of land vanish, their hearts sank, and they shed bitter tears, weeping for home and the loved ones they thought never more to see.

On and on they sailed, and as day after day no land appeared, the men grew restless. Seeing them thus restless, and lest they should be utterly terrified at being so far from home upon this seemingly endless waste of waters, Columbus determined to keep them from knowing how far they had really gone. So he kept two reckonings. One, in which the real length of the ships' daily journey was given, he kept to himself; the other, in which the journey was given as much shorter, he showed to the sailors.

A month went past, six weeks went past, and still there was no trace of land. Then at length came signs. Snowbirds which never ventured far to sea flew round the ships. Now the waves bore to them a rudely carved stick, now the ships ploughed a way through masses of floating weeds. All these signs were at first greeted with joy and hope, and the sailors took heart. But as still the days went past and no land appeared, they lost heart again.

The fields of weeds which they had at first greeted with joy now became an added terror. Would they not be caught in this tangle of weeds, they asked, and never more win a way out of it? To their fearful and superstitious minds, the very breeze which had borne them softly onward became a menace. For if the wind always blew steadily from the east, how was it possible ever to return to Spain? So Columbus was almost glad when a contrary wind blew. For it proved to his trembling sailors that one, at least, of their fears was groundless. But it made little difference. The men were now utterly given over to gloomy terrors.

Fear robbed them of all ambition. Ferdinand and Isabella had promised a large sum of money to the man who should first discover land. But none cared now to win it. All they desired was to turn home once more.

Fear made them mutinous also. So they whispered together and planned in secret to rid themselves of Columbus. It would be easy, they thought, to throw him overboard some dark night, and then give out that he had fallen into the sea by accident. No one would know. No one in Spain would care, for Columbus was, after all, but a foreigner and an upstart. The great ocean would keep the secret. They would be free to turn homeward.

Columbus saw their dark looks, heard the murmurs of the crews, and did his best to hearten them again. He spoke to them cheerfully, persuading and encouraging, yet all the while it was to him a time of weeping in his heart.

Still the men went sullenly about their work. But at length one morning, a sudden cry from the *Pinta* shook them from out their sullen thoughts.

It was the captain of the *Pinta* who shouted. "Land, land, my lord!" he cried. "I claim the reward."

And when Columbus heard that shout, his heart was filled with joy and thankfulness, and baring his head he sank upon his knees, giving praise to God. The crew followed his example. Then, their hearts suddenly light and joyous, they swarmed up the masts and into the rigging to feast their eyes upon the goodly sight.

All day they sailed onward toward the promised land. The sun sank, and still all night the ships sped on their joyous way. But when morning dawned, the land seemed no nearer than before. Hope died away again, and sorrowfully as the day went on, the woeful truth that the fancied land had been but a bank of clouds was forced upon Columbus.

Again for days the ships sailed on, and as still no land appeared, the men again began to murmur. Then one day when Columbus walked on deck he was met, not merely with sullen looks, but with angry words. The men clamored to return. And if the Admiral refused, why, so much the worse for him. They would endure no longer.

Bravely the Admiral faced the mutineers. He talked to them cheerfully. He reminded them of what honor and gain would be theirs when they returned home, having found the new way to India, of what wealth they might win by trading. Then he ended sternly:

"Complain how you may," he said. "I have to go to the Indies, and I will go on till I find them, so help me God."

For the time being, the Admiral's stern, brave words cowed the mutineers. But not for much longer, Columbus knew right well, would they obey him if land did not soon appear. And in his heart, he prayed God that it might not be long delayed.

The next night Columbus stood alone upon the poop deck of the *Santa Maria*. Full of anxious thoughts, he gazed out into the darkness. Then suddenly it seemed to him that far in the distance, he saw a glimmering light appear and disappear once and again. It was as if someone walking carried a light. But so fearful was Columbus lest his fervent hopes had caused him to imagine this light, that he would not trust his own eyes alone. So he called to one of his officers and asked him if he saw any light.

"Yes," replied the officer. "I see a light."

Then Columbus called a second man. He could not at first see the light, and in any case neither of them thought much of it. Columbus, however, made sure that land was close, and calling the men about him he bade them keep a sharp lookout, promising a silken doublet to the man who should first see land.

So till two o'clock in the morning the ships held on their way. Then from the *Pinta,* there came again a joyful shout of "Land! Land!"

This time it proved no vision, it was land, indeed; and at last, the long-looked-for goal was reached. The land proved to be an island covered with beautiful trees, and as they neared the shore, the sailors saw tall men of the Taino tribe, crowding to the beach.

In awed wonder, these men watched the huge white birds, as the ships with their great sails seemed to them. Nearer and nearer they came, and when they reached the shore and folded their wings, the Taino fled to the shelter of the forest. But seeing that they were not pursued, their curiosity got the better of their fear, and returning again they stood in silent astonishment to watch the Spaniards land.

First of all came Columbus. Over his glittering steel armor he wore a rich cloak of scarlet, and in his hand he bore the Royal Standard of Spain. Then, each at the head of his own ship's crew, came the captains of the *Pinta* and the *Niña,* each carrying in his hand a white banner with a green cross and the crowned initials of the King and Queen, which was the special banner devised for the great adventure. Every man was dressed in his best, and the brightly-colored clothes, the shining armor, and fluttering banners made a striking pageant. Upon it the sun shone in splendor and the blue sky was reflected in a bluer sea, while startled scarlet flamingoes rose in brilliant flight.

As Columbus landed, he fell upon his knees and kissed the ground, and with tears of joy running down his cheeks, he gave thanks to God, the whole company following his example. Then rising again to his feet, Columbus drew his sword, and solemnly took possession of the island in the name of Ferdinand and Isabella.

When the ceremony was over, the crew burst forth into shouts of triumph and joy. They crowded round Columbus, kneeling before him to kiss his hands and feet, praying forgiveness for their insolence and mutiny, and promising in the future to obey him without question. For Columbus, it was a moment of pure joy and triumph. All his long years of struggle and waiting had come to a glorious end.

Yet he knew already that his search was not finished, his triumph not yet complete. He had not reached the eastern shores of India, the land of spice and pearls. He had not even reached Cipango, the rich and golden isle. But he had at least, he thought, found some outlying island off the coast of India, and that India itself could not be far away. He never discovered his mistake, so the group of islands nowhere near India, but lying between the two great Continents of America, are known as the West Indies, and Columbus later called the inhabitants thereof "Indians."

Columbus called the island upon which he first landed San Salvador, and for a long time it was thought to be the island which is still called San Salvador or Cat Island. But lately people have come to believe that Columbus first landed upon an island a little further south, now called Watling Island.

From San Salvador, Columbus sailed about and landed upon several other islands, naming them and taking possession of them for Spain. He saw many strange and beautiful fruits: as he wrote in his journal, "There are trees of a thousand sorts, and all have their several fruits; and I feel the most unhappy man in the world not to know them, for I am well assured that they are all valuable." He saw flocks of beautifully colored parrots and many other birds that sang most sweetly. He saw fair harbors so safe and spacious that he thought they might hold all the ships of the world.

But of such things Columbus was not in search. He was seeking for gold and jewels, and at every place he touched he hoped to find some great eastern potentate, robed in splendor and seated upon a golden throne; instead everywhere he found only the Taino people. They were friendly and gentle, and what gold they had - but it was little indeed - they willingly bartered for a few glass beads, or little tinkling bells.

By signs, however, some of these Tainos made Columbus understand that further south there was a great king who was so wealthy that he ate off dishes of wrought gold. Others told him of a land where the people gathered gold on the beach at nighttime by the light of torches; others again told him of a land where gold was so common that the people wore it on their arms and legs, and in their ears and noses as ornaments. Others still told of islands where there was more gold than earth. In his desire for gold, Columbus forced the Tainos to lead him to these treasures, but the search was in vain.

In his cruisings Columbus sailed to Cuba, and thought at first it must be the island of Cipango, but finding himself mistaken he decided at length that he had landed upon the most easterly point of India. He could not be far, he thought, from the palace of the Grand Khan, and choosing out two of his company he sent them as ambassadors to him. But after six days the ambassadors returned, having found no gold; and instead of the Grand Khan, having seen only a chieftain.

These ambassadors found no gold, but had they only known it, they found something quite as valuable. For they told how they had met men and women with fire-brands in their hands made of herbs, the end of which they put in their mouths and sucked, blowing forth smoke. And these fire-brands they called *tabacos*.

The Spaniards also discovered that the inhabitants of these islands used for food a root which they dug out of the earth. But they thought nothing of these things. For what were roots and dried herbs to those who came in search of gold, and gems, and precious spices? So they brought home neither potatoes nor tobacco.

So far the three little vessels had kept together, but now the captain of the *Pinta* parted company with the others, not owing to bad weather, says Columbus in his diary, but "in disobedience to and against the wish of the Admiral, and out of avarice, thinking that an Indian who had been put on board his caravel could show him where there was much gold." This desertion grieved Columbus greatly, for he feared that Pinzon might find gold first, and sailing home before him, cheat him of all the honor and glory of the quest. Still the Admiral did not give up but continued to steer his course in the name of God and in search of gold and spices, and to discover land.

So from island to island he went seeking gold, and finding everywhere gentle, kindly people, fair birds and flowers, and stately trees.

Notes:

A silken doublet was an article of clothing.

The Taino were an Arawak people that inhabited several islands in the

Caribbean Sea at the time of Columbus' arrival. Their ancestors originally came from South America.

Cipango was Marco Polo's name for Japan.

After 1925, Watling Island was called San Salvador Island. The other island was called Cat Island. Both islands are a part of the Bahamas.

Some passages in this chapter are taken from The Life and Voyages of Christopher Columbus, *by Washington Irving, 1828.*

"There are trees of a thousand sorts" quote is from Journal of Christopher Columbus (During his first voyage, 1492-93), *Sunday, 21st of October.*

"In disobedience to and against the wish of the Admiral" quote is from the same journal, Wednesday, 21st of November.

Pronunciation Guide:

Taino – TAY-no

Chapter 4

How Columbus Returned Home in Triumph

Christmas Eve came, and the Admiral, being very weary, went below to sleep, leaving a sailor to steer the ship. But this sailor thought he, too, would like to sleep, so he gave the tiller in charge of a boy.

Now throughout the whole voyage, the Admiral had forbidden this. Whether it was stormy or calm, he had commanded that the helm was never to be entrusted to a boy. This boy knew very little of how to steer a ship, and being caught in a current, it was cast upon a sandbank and wrecked. By good luck, everyone was saved and landed upon the island of Haiti. But Columbus had now only one little vessel, and it was not large enough to carry all the company. Many of them, however, were so delighted with the islands that they wanted to stay there, and they had often asked the Admiral's leave to do so.

Columbus, therefore, now determined to allow some of his men to remain to found a little colony, and trade with the Taino, and "he trusted in God that, when he returned from Spain, according to his intention, he would find a ton of gold collected by barter by those he was to leave behind, and that they would have found the mine, and spices in such quantities that the Sovereigns would, in three years, be able to undertake and fit out an expedition to go and conquer the Holy Sepulchre."

So out of the wreck of the *Santa Maria*, Columbus built a fort, and from the many who begged to be left behind he chose forty-four, appointing one of them, Diego de Arana, as Governor. He called the fort La Navidad, or The Nativity, in memory of the day upon which it was founded. The island itself he called Española, or Little Spain.

Then on Friday, the 4th of January 1493, the *Niña* spread her sails and slowly glided away, leaving these settlers in that far island amid the unknown seas.

Two days after Columbus set forth upon his homeward voyage, he fell in again with the *Pinta*. The master had found no gold, so he determined to join Columbus once more. He now came on board and tried to make his peace with Columbus, but the Admiral received him coldly, for he had little faith in his excuses. And now once more together, the two little vessels sailed homeward. But soon storms arose, the ships were battered by wind, tossed about hither and thither by waves, and at length separated again. More than once, Columbus feared that his tiny vessel would be engulfed in the stormy seas, and the results of his great enterprise never be known. But at length the shores of Portugal were sighted, and on Friday, the 15th of March 1493, he landed again at Palos, in Spain, from whence he had set forth more than seven months before.

The people of Palos had hardly hoped to see again those who had sailed away on so desperate an adventure. Now, when they saw only one of the three vessels return, their joy was mingled with grief. When, however, they learned that Columbus returned in triumph, and that India had been reached, their joy knew no bounds. Shops were closed, bells were rung, and all the people in holiday attire thronged to the harbor, and with shouts and cheers they bore Columbus in triumph to the church, there to give thanks to God for his safe and glorious return. And ere the shouts had died away, a second vessel was seen approaching. It was the *Pinta* which, though parted from the *Niña*, had also weathered the storms and now came safely to port.

At once on landing, Columbus had sent a letter to the King and Queen telling them of his return. Now he received an answer; it was addressed to Don Christopher Columbus, our Admiral of the Ocean Sea, Viceroy and Governor of the Islands discovered in the Indies. It bade him to come at once to court. It told him that a new expedition would immediately be fitted out; so with a heart overflowing with joy and pride, Columbus set forth to Barcelona where the King and Queen then were.

The great news of his voyage and discovery had outsped him, and the people of Barcelona received him with every mark of respect and honor. As he passed through the streets, riding on a splendid horse and surrounded by the greatest nobles of Spain, they cheered him again and again. They gazed in wonder also at the Taino captives he took with him from out the Sea of Darkness, and the brightly colored parrots they carried in cages.

Sitting on a throne of state beneath a canopy of cloth of gold, with the young Prince of Spain beside them, the King and Queen received Columbus. At his approach they rose, and standing they welcomed back to their realm as a mighty prince he who had gone forth a simple sailor. And as Columbus would have knelt to kiss their hands, they raised him and bade him be seated beside them as an equal. Seldom did the haughty rulers of Spain show such great honor even to the proudest nobles in the land.

And so while King and Queen and courtiers listened breathlessly, Columbus told of all he had done, of all the marvels he had seen, of the richness and fairness of the lands he had found and claimed for Spain. And when he had finished, the King and Queen fell upon their knees, and clasping their hands, they raised eyes filled with tears of joy to heaven, giving thanks to God for His great mercies. The courtiers, too, fell upon their knees and joined their prayers to those of the King and Queen, while over all the triumphant notes of the Te Deum rang out.

So ended the first great voyage of Columbus. He had shown the way across the Sea of Darkness; he had proved that all the stories of its monsters and other dangers were false. But even he had no idea of the importance of his accomplishment. He never realized that he had shown the way to a new world; he believed to the day of his death that he had indeed found new islands, but that his greatest feat was that of finding a new way to the Old World. Yet now being made a noble, he took for his coat of arms a group of golden islands in an azure sea, and for motto the words, "To Castile and Leon, Columbus gave a New World."

Now began a time of pomp and splendor for Columbus. He who had gone forth a penniless sailor now rode abroad in gorgeous array; often he might be seen with the Queen on one hand, and John, the young Prince of Spain, on the other. Sometimes even the King himself would ride with him, and seeing him so high in royal favor, all the greatest and proudest nobles of the land were eager to make much of him. So they fêted him, flattered him, and spread banquets for him. But some were jealous of the great fame of Columbus, and they made light of his accomplishments.

It is told how, one day at a banquet when everyone talked of these wonderful deeds, one of the guests spoke slightingly of them. "It is all very well," he said to Columbus, "but in a great country like Spain, where there are such numbers of daring sailors and learned folk besides, many another man might have done the same as you. We should have found the Indies even if you had not."

To this speech Columbus answered nothing, but he asked for an egg to be brought to him. When it was brought, he placed it on the table saying, "Sirs, I will lay a wager with any of you that you cannot make this egg stand up without anything at all to support it."

One after the other they tried, but no one could do it. At length it came round to Columbus again. And he, taking it in his hand, struck it sharply on the table so that one end was chipped a little, and it stood upright.

"That, my lord, is my answer," he said, looking at the courtier who had scoffed. And all the company were silent. For they saw he was well answered. Columbus had shown that after a deed is once done it is simple, and everyone knows how to do it. What he had done in sailing across the Sea of Darkness was only wonderful because no one else had thought of doing it.

Portugal was now very jealous of Spain's success, and King Ferdinand of Spain was fearful lest King John of Portugal should seize the new islands which Columbus had discovered. So he appealed to the Pope to settle the matter. And the Pope decided that all new lands reached west of an imaginary line drawn through the Atlantic Ocean west of the Azores and from pole to pole should belong to Spain. All discoveries east of this line should belong to Portugal. If you will look at a map of the world you will see that this gave to Spain all the Americas with their islands (except a little bit of Brazil), and to Portugal the whole of Africa.

But almost before this matter was settled, Columbus had set forth again on another voyage across the great ocean, now no longer the Sea of Darkness. This time he had no difficulty in getting a company. For everyone was eager to go with him, even many of the sons of great nobles. This time, too, the passage was made without any doubts and fears, but with joyful expectations.

Columbus had hoped great things of the little colony that he had left behind him. But when he cast anchor one night before the fort, his heart sank. All was dark and silent on shore. Yet still hoping, he ordered two cannons to be fired as a signal to the colonists. The cannons boomed through the still, warm darkness of the night, and slowly the echoes died away. But there was no answer, save the sighing of the sea and the scream of the startled birds. From the fort there came no sound or any sign of life, and with sad forebodings, the Spaniards waited for the dawn.

Then it was seen that the fort was a ruin. It had been burned and sacked. Torn clothing and broken vessels were strewn around, but as the Spaniards wandered sadly among the ruins, they found no trace of their companions, save eleven graves with the grass growing above them.

At first none of the Taino people would speak to Columbus and his men, for they feared their anger. But at length, tempted by the offer of gifts and other friendly signs, they came. They told how the Spaniards had first quarreled amongst themselves, then how the fort had been attacked by Native people from another island, and how all of Columbus' men had been slain.

Thus ended the first European colony ever planted in Western lands. All traces of it have vanished, and upon the spot where La Navidad stood, there is now a little fishing village called Petit Anse.

Columbus founded other colonies, but they succeeded no better than the first one. In all, Columbus made four voyages across the

Atlantic, and in the third he landed upon the coast of South America, near the mouth of the Orinoco. But Columbus did not know that at last he had come upon the great double Continent of America. He thought that he had merely reached another island, and he named it La Isla Santa. Afterwards he was so delighted at the beauty of the land that he thought he must have found the Garden of Eden, so he became certain that he had landed on the eastern corner of Asia.

During these later voyages, Columbus exacted forced labor and taxes from the people, and there were harsh and severe penalties for failure. The island population was greatly reduced. This was because of a great lack of food, the punitive treatment by Columbus' men, and the new diseases that Columbus and his crew brought with their voyages. Many other captured Tainos were sent to Spain to be sold as slaves.

In 1506, Columbus died. He who, by his great faith and great daring, led the way across the Sea of Darkness, and gave a New World to the Old, died in poverty and neglect. The men who had wept for joy at the news of his discovery shed no tear over his grave. Years passed before men recognized what a great man had dwelt among them: years passed before any monument was raised to his memory. But indeed he had scarce need of any, for as an American writer said, "The New World is his monument." And every child of the New World must surely honor that land and seek never to deface it.

Notes:

A "Te Deum" is a Latin hymn, which begins "Te Deum laudamus": "We praise Thee, O God."

Some passages in this chapter are from Journal of Christopher Columbus, December 26, 1492.

The last quote is from Justin Winsor, Christopher Columbus and how he received and imparted the spirit of discovery, *1891.*

Pronunciation Guide:

Te Deum – TEE or TAY DEE-um
Isla – In Spanish, it is pronounced EES-la

Chapter 5

How America Was Named

"The New World is his monument." And yet the New World does not bear the name of Columbus. So in this chapter I am going to tell you how America was named.

As soon as Columbus had shown the way across the Sea of Darkness, many were eager to follow in his footsteps. "But now there is not a man," he says himself, "down to the very tailors, who does not beg to become a discoverer." Among the many who longed to sail the seas, there was a man named Amerigo Vespucci.

Like Columbus, Amerigo Vespucci was an Italian. He was born in Florence, and there for nearly forty years he lived quietly, earning his living as a clerk in the great merchant house of Medici. But although he was diligent at business, his thoughts were not wholly taken up with it, and in his leisure hours, he loved to read books of geography and pore over maps and charts.

After a time, business took Amerigo to Spain. He was there when Columbus returned from his famous first voyage, and very likely saw him pass through the streets of Barcelona on his day of triumph. Just when Amerigo and Columbus met, we do not know. But very soon we find Amerigo in the service of the merchant who supplied Columbus with food and other necessaries for his second voyage. It has been thought by some that Vespucci went with Columbus on this voyage, but that is not very likely. It was about this time, however, that Vespucci went on his first voyage in which he explored the coast of Venezuela or of Central America. It is very doubtful which. Before going on this voyage, he had been in Spain about four years, and not having succeeded very well as a merchant, he decided to give up trading and take to a sea life.

No voyages perhaps have been more written about and fought over than those of Amerigo Vespucci. Some will have it that he went on only two voyages, and they say he was a braggart and a vainglorious fool if he said he went more. Others think that he went on at least four voyages. And most people are now agreed that he who gave his name to the great double Continent of America was no swaggering pretender, but a genuine explorer.

In the first two voyages that he made, Vespucci sailed under the flag of Spain. In the second two, he sailed in the service of the King of Portugal. But after his fourth voyage, he returned again to Spain. There he received a large salary and the rank of captain. Later he was made Pilot Major of Spain and was held in high honor until his death.

Yet in all the voyages Vespucci went, whether under the flag of Portugal or of Spain, he was never leader. He went as astronomer, or as pilot, while other men captained the expeditions.

It is from Amerigo's letters alone that we gather the little we know about his voyages. For although he says in one of his letters that he has written a book called *The Four Voyages*, it has never been found, and perhaps was never published. One long letter, however, which he wrote to an old schoolfellow was so interesting that it was published and read by many people all over Europe. It was, says Sir Thomas More, "abroad in every man's hands."

Amerigo's voyages led him chiefly to Central and South America, and he became convinced that South America was a continent. So soon, what with the voyages of Vespucci and the voyages of other great men, it became at last quite certain that there was a vast continent beyond the Atlantic Ocean. Mapmakers, therefore, began to draw a huge island, large enough to form in itself a continent, south of the Equator. They called it the New World, or the land of the Holy Cross, but the Northern Continent was still represented on the maps by a few small islands, or as a part of Asia.

Thus years passed. Daring sailors still sailed the stormy seas in search of new lands, and learned men read the tales of their adventures and wrote new books of geography.

Then one day a professor who taught geography at the Monastery of St. Dié in Alsace published a little book on geography. In it he spoke of Europe, Asia, and Africa, the three parts of the world as known to the ancients. Then he spoke of the fourth part which had been discovered by Amerigo Vespucci, by which he meant what we now call South America. "And," continues this professor, "I do not see what is rightly to hinder us from calling it Amerige or America, that is, the land of Americus, after its discoverer."

This is the first time the word America was ever used, and little did this old German professor, writing in his quiet Alsatian College, think that he was christening the great double continent of the New World. And as little did Amerigo think in writing his letter to his old school fellow that he was to be looked upon as the discoverer of the New World.

At first the new name came slowly into use, and it appears for the first time on a map made about 1514. In this map, America is shown as a great island continent lying chiefly south of the Equator.

All the voyages which Columbus had made had been north of the Equator. No man yet connected the land south of the Equator with him, and it was at first only to this south land that the name America was given.

Thirty years and more went by. Many voyages were made, and it became known for certain that Columbus had not reached the shores of India by sailing west, and that a great Continent barred the way north as well as south of the Equator.

Then a famous mapmaker gave the name of America to both continents.

But many Spaniards were jealous for the fame of Columbus, and they thought that the Northern Continent should be called Colonia or Columbiana. One, anxious that the part in the discovery taken by Ferdinand and Isabella should not be forgotten, even tried to make people call it Fer-Isabelica.

But all such efforts were in vain. America sounded well, people liked it, and soon everyone used it.

Amerigo Vespucci himself had nothing to do with the choice, and yet because others gave his name to the New World, many hard things have been said of him. He has been called in scorn a "land lubber," "a beef and biscuit contractor," and other contemptuous names. Even one of the greatest American writers has poured scorn on him. "Strange," Ralph Waldo Emerson says, "that broad America must wear the name of a thief. Amerigo Vespucci, the pickle dealer of Seville ... whose highest naval rank was a boatswain's mate in an expedition that never sailed, managed in this lying world to supplant Columbus, and baptize half the earth with his own dishonest name."

But it was the people of his day, and not Vespucci, who brought the new name into use. Vespucci himself had never any intention of being a thief or of robbing Columbus of his glory. He and Columbus had always been friends, and little more than a year before he died,

Columbus wrote a letter to his son Diego which Vespucci delivered. In this letter Columbus says, "Amerigo Vespucci, the bearer of this letter ... was always desirous of pleasing me. He is a very honourable man....He goes for me, and is very desirous of doing something to benefit me if it is in his power."

It was only accident which gave the name of America to the New World, and perhaps also the ingratitude of the great leader's own generation.

Later generations, however, have not been so unmindful of Columbus and his deeds; Americans have not allowed his name to be wholly forgotten. The district in which the capital of the United States is situated is called Columbia. In Canada, too, there is the great province of British Columbia, and in South America the United States of Colombia, besides many towns all named in honor of the great discoverer.

Notes:

Some quotes in this chapter are attributed as follows:

Columbus' quote "But now there is not a man" comes from his letter to Ferdinand and Isabella about his fourth voyage, quoted in Justin Winsor's

book Christopher Columbus and How He Received and Imparted the Spirit of Discovery, *1892.*

Sir Thomas More's quote is from Utopia, *in one of the translations.*

The professor's quote is from Martin Waldseemuller, Introduction to Cosmography, *1507.*

Ralph Waldo Emerson's quote is from English Traits, *1856.*

Columbus' letter to his son is dated February 5, 1505.

Pronunciation Guide:

Amerigo Vespucci – am-mare-EE-go veh-SPOO-chee

Chapter 6

How the Flag of England Was Planted on the Shores of the New World

Christopher Columbus showed the way across the Sea of Darkness; Amerigo Vespucci gave his name to the great double Continent. But it was another Italian, Giovanni Caboto, known as John Cabot, who landed on the Continent of North America.

Like Columbus, Cabot was born in Genoa. When, however, he left his own land, he did not go to Spain like Columbus, but to England.

He had been living in England for some years when the news of the first great voyage of Columbus was brought there. Soon everyone was talking about the wonderful discovery, from the King and his court downward.

Cabot was a trader and a daring sailor, well used to sailing on the stormy seas. Yet even he was awed by what Columbus had done. To find that way never known before, and by sailing west to reach the east "where the spices grow" seemed to him "a thing more divine than human." And he, too, longed to follow Columbus, and maybe encounter new lands.

King Henry VII was eager to claim new lands as the Kings of Spain and Portugal were doing. So he listened to the persuasions of John Cabot. And in spite of the Pope - who had divided all the undiscovered world between the Kings of Spain and Portugal—the King gave him leave "to sail to all parts, regions and coasts of the eastern, western and northern sea" and to plant the banner of England upon any "islands,

countries, regions or provinces of heathens and infidels, in whatsoever part of the world placed, which before this time were unknown to
all Christians." He bade his "well beloved John Cabot" take five ships
and set forth on the adventure at his "own proper costs and charges."
For Henry was a King "wise and not lavish," and although he wanted
England to have the glory of new discoveries, he was not eager to
spend his gold on them.

But where could a poor sailor find money enough for so great an
adventure?

So a year went past, and although Cabot had the King's leave to go,
he did not set out. But he did not let the King forget. And at length,
close-fisted Henry listened to "the busy request and supplication" of
the eager sailor and consented to fit out one small ship.

So at five o'clock one sweet May morning, a frail little vessel called
the *Matthew*, with a crew of but eighteen men, sailed out from Bristol
harbor. Many people came to see the vessel sail. For they were nearly
all Bristol men who were thus venturing forth on the unknown deep,
and their friends crowded to the harbor to wish them Godspeed.

It was a great occasion for Bristol, and indeed for all England, for
it was the first voyage of discovery with which the English king and
people had to do. So the tiny white-sailed ship put out to sea, followed
by the prayers and wishes of those left behind. With tear-dimmed eyes,
they watched it till it faded from view. Then they turned homewards
to pray for the return of their loved ones.

Round the coast of Ireland the vessel sped. But at last its green
shores faded from sight, and the little company of eighteen brave men
were alone upon the trackless waves.

Westward and ever westward they sailed, as the Canadian poet
Wilfred Campbell wrote,

"Over the hazy distance,
  Beyond the sunset's rim."

Week after week went by. Six weeks and then seven, and still no
land appeared. Those were days of anxiety and gloom. But still the
hope of the golden west lured Cabot on, and at length one day in June,
he heard the glad cry of "Land! Land!"

So on St. John's Day in 1497, John Cabot landed somewhere on the coast of America. He called the land Prima Tierra Vista or First Land Seen, and because of the day upon which it was found, he called an island near to it St. John's Isle.

We cannot tell exactly where Cabot cast anchor; it may have been at Cape Breton or somewhere on the coast of Labrador. But wherever it was that he landed, he there set up a great cross and unfurled the flag of England, claiming the land for King Henry.

When Cabot set out, he was full of the ideas of Columbus. He had hoped to find himself on the coast of Asia and in the land of gold and spices. Now he knew himself mistaken. He did not see any people, but he knew the land was inhabited, for he found notched trees, snares for wild animals, and other signs of habitation which he took home.

He had found no cities of gold, he had had speech with no stately potentate. Yet he was not utterly disappointed. For the country he had found seemed to him fair and fertile, and the quantities of fish which swarmed in the seas amazed both himself and his men. They had no need of lines or even of nets. They had but to let down a basket weighted with a stone and draw it up again to have all the fish they wanted.

Cabot stayed but a short time in the new-found land. He would fain have stayed longer and explored further, but he feared lest his provisions would give out, and so regretfully he turned homeward.

Great was the excitement in Bristol when the tiny ship came to anchor there once more, little more than three months after it had sailed away. And so strange were the tales Master Cabot had to tell that the folk of Bristol would hardly have believed him (for he was a poor man and a foreigner) had not his crew of honest Bristol men vouched for the truth of all he said. Everyone was delighted. Even thrifty King Henry was so much pleased that he gave Cabot ten pounds. It seems a small enough sum "to hym that found the new isle." But we must remember that it would be worth much more than that today.

Cabot, at any rate, found it enough with which to buy a suit of silk. And dressed in this new splendor, he walked about the streets of Bristol followed by gaping crowds. He was now called the Great Admiral, and much honor was paid to him. Everyone was eager to talk with him, eager to go with him on his next voyage: and that even although they knew that many of the crew would be thieves and evildoers. For the King had promised to give Cabot for sailors all prisoners except those who were confined for high treason.

We know little more of John Cabot. Later King Henry gave him a pension of 20 pounds a year. It seems likely that the following year he set out again across the broad Atlantic, taking his sons with him. "The rest is silence."

How John Cabot ended his life, where he lies taking his rest, we do not know.

"He sleeps somewhere in sod unknown,
Without a slab, without a stone."

We remember him chiefly because he was the first to lead Englishmen across the Atlantic, and the first to plant the flag of England upon the Continent of North America, which, in days to come, was to be the home of two great English-speaking peoples.

Notes:

"Where the spices grow" is from **John and Sebastian Cabot,**"*by Francesco Tarducci and Henry Francis Brownson, 1893.*

"A thing more divine" is from **A Memoir of Sebastian Cabot: With a Review of the History of Maritime Discovery,**"*Richard Biddle, 1831.*

Quotes about "Well beloved" through "islands, countries, regions" are from letters patent from Henry VII to John Cabot and his sons, March 5, 1496.

The quote about Henry VII ("wise and not lavish") is from Collections of the Maine Historical Society, 1897, a footnote from a letter of Raimondo to the Duke of Milan under date of December 18, 1497; also found in the Hakluyt Society's edition of the journal of Christopher Columbus (which quotes it as "wise and not prodigal").

"The busy request and supplication" is from **John and Sebastian Cabot: The Discovery of North America,** *by Charles Raymond Beazley, 1898.*

The poem entitled "Sebastian Cabot" is by Canadian poet William Wilfred Campbell, included in the book **Beyond the Hills of Dream.**

Regarding pounds: "Prior to the Coinage Act of 1792, which established the dollar, the English pound was the primary form of currency in colonial America. The pound—which, in the Middle Ages, was valued the same as one pound of sterling silver—had 20 shillings, and each shilling had 12 pence (pennies). (The modern pound follows the decimal system and, since 1971, has been divided into 100 pence.)" *From https://vitabrevis. americanancestors.org/2015/02/making-sense-money-colonial-america/*

"To hym that found a new isle" is from an entry of the 10th August, 1497, Privy Purse accounts of Henry VII.

"The rest is silence" is a quote from Shakespeare's **Hamlet***.*

"He sleeps somewhere in sod unknown" is from Campbell's poem.

Chapter 7

How the Flag of France Was Planted in Florida

As years went on, many voyages of discovery and exploration were made to the New World by both the Spaniards and the Portuguese, but chiefly by the Spaniards. America was the land of golden hopes and the land of splendid adventure, and the haughty knights of Spain, thirsting for gold and for fame, were lured thither. They sought the fabled seven cities of gold, they sought the fountain of eternal youth. Through the dark pathless forests, across the wide prairies, they flashed in glittering array, awaking the vast silences with the clash of arms. They came in all the pomp and splendor of warfare; they brought also the Cross of Christ, threatening the inhabitants with death if they did not bow to Him and be baptized. And it seemed for a time as if they, and they only, would possess the vast continent. But expedition after expedition ended in disaster. The Spaniards found neither the far-famed seven cities nor the fountain of youth. And many of the Native people, instead of accepting their forced religion, hated them and it with a deep hatred.

But the Spaniards were not long left in undisputed possession of America. The French King, too, desired to have new lands across the seas, and he saw no reason why Spain and Portugal should divide the New World between them.

"What," Francis I said, "shall the Kings of Spain and Portugal quietly divide all America between them, without suffering me to take a share as their brother? I would fain see the article in father Adam's will, which bequeaths that vast inheritance to them."

From France, therefore, daring men sailed forth to the New World. And there they set up the arms of their country, claiming broad lands for their King.

And now came the time when all of Europe was torn asunder by religious strife. The Protestant Reformation had begun, and everywhere there was discord between the people who followed the old religion and those who followed the new. In France, those who followed the new religion were called Huguenots. They were often harshly treated and were denied the freedom to worship God in their own way. Many of them, therefore, longed to get away from France and go to some new country where they would have the freedom they desired.

So a few grave, stern men gathered together and determined to set out for some place in the New World where they might make a home and where they could worship God freely.

Then one February day in 1562, two little ships sailed away from France. Westward they sailed, until about two and a half months later they landed in what is now Florida.

It was May Day, the sun shone and all the world seemed bright and green, and these Protestant adventurers thought they had never seen so fair a land. It was, they said, "the fairest, frutefullest and pleasantest of all the worlds," "abounding in honey, venison and wildfowl." They encountered the friendly Timucua people, who told the newcomers by signs that the seven golden cities were not far off. That rejoiced their hearts, for even those stern old Huguenots were not above following the quest for gold.

Here then in this far-off land, the Huguenots set up a stone pillar carved with the arms of the King of France. And kneeling round it, they gave thanks to God for having brought them to so fair a country. Then returning to their ships, they sailed northward along the coast. For they had not come to settle, but merely to explore, and find out a good spot on which to found a colony.

But the land seemed so fair, the air so balmy, that they were ready to settle there at once, and never return to France.

At length after inspecting several places, the adventurers reached a spot not far from what is now Beaufort in South Carolina. Here they landed, and knowing that many of the men were already eager to remain in this beautiful country, Jean Ribault, their leader, resolved to found a colony. So he called them all together, and speaking wise and brave words to them, asked who among them would remain.

"Declare your minds freely unto me," he said, "that your renown shall hereafter shine unquenchable through our realm of France."

Ribault had scarcely finished speaking when nearly all the men replied with a shout, "We ask nothing better than to remain in this beautiful country."

Indeed so many were anxious to remain that Ribault had enough to do to persuade a sufficient number to man the ships to return with him.

In the end, nearly thirty men were chosen to remain. At once they set about building a fort which they called Charlesfort in honor of the boy King, Charles IX, who was then upon the throne.

The men worked so well that in a very few days the fort was so far finished that it was fit to live in. Food and ammunition were brought from the ships, and a man named Albert de la Pierria was chosen as Governor. Then for the last time, Ribault gathered all the men together and took leave of those to be left behind.

"Captain Albert," he said, "I have to request you, in the presence of all men, that you would quit yourself so wisely in your charge, that I never have occasion but to commend you unto the king.

"And you, companions," he said, turning to the soldiers, "I beseech you also to esteem Captain Albert as if it were myself that stayed here with you, yielding to him that obedience which a soldier oweth unto his general and captain, living as brethren one with another without all dissension, and in so doing God will assist you and bless your enterprises."

Then farewells were said, and Ribault sailed away, leaving the chosen men alone in the wilderness.

From north to south, from east to west, in all the vast continent there were no Europeans save themselves. The little company was made up of young nobles, sailors, merchants, and artisans. There were no farmers or peasants among them, and when they had finished their fort, none of them thought of clearing the land and sowing corn. There was no need: Ribault would soon return, they thought, bringing with him all they required. So they made friends with the Native people, and roamed the forest wilds in search of gold and of adventures, without care for the future.

But the days and weeks passed, and Ribault did not return. For when he arrived home, he found that France was torn with civil war between the Roman Catholics and the Protestant Huguenots, and that it was impossible to get ships fitted out to sail to America.

Soon the little colony began to feel the pangs of hunger. Daily they scanned the pitiless blue sea for a glimpse of Ribault's returning sail. No sail appeared, and daily their supplies dwindled away. Had it not been for the friendly Native people, they might all have perished. For the Indians were generous, and as long as they had food themselves, they shared it with their new friends. But at length they could spare no more. Indeed they had already given the Frenchmen so much food that they themselves, they said, would be forced to roam the woods in search of roots and herbs to keep them from starving until harvest was ripe. They told the Frenchmen, however, of two rich and powerful chiefs who held sway over land which lay to the south, where they might obtain endless supplies of corn and vegetables.

This was indeed good news to the Frenchmen. And guided by their Indian friends, they lost no time in setting out to beg food from these potentates.

When the Frenchmen reached the home of one of these chiefs, they were received with great honor. They found that their friends had spoken truly. Here there was food in abundance; and after a great feast they returned joyfully to the fort, carrying with them a great supply of corn and beans, and - what was still better - a promise from the friendly chief that he would give them more food whenever they had need of it.

Once more the colonists rejoiced in plenty. But not for long. For the very night they arrived home their storehouse took fire, and all the food which they had brought with such joy was destroyed.

Again famine stared them in the face. In their plight they once more appealed to the chief who supplied their wants as generously as before, promising them that as long as his meal should last they should never want. So for the time being, the colonists were saved from starvation.

But another danger now threatened them, for quarrels arose among the men. Albert de Pierria, who had been set over them as captain, proved to be cruel and despotic. He oppressed the men in many ways, hanging and imprisoning at will those who displeased him. Soon the men began to murmur under his tyranny. Dark looks greeted Albert de Pierria: he answered them with darker deeds. At length one day for some misdeed, he banished a soldier to a lonely island, and left him there to die of hunger. This was more than the colonists could well bear. Their smoldering anger burst forth, and seizing the tyrant, they put him to death. Then they chose one of their number called Nicolas Barre to be their captain.

They were rid of their tyrant, and that brought peace for a time to the little colony. But the men had grown to hate the place. The land which had once seemed to them so fair now seemed no better than a prison, and they longed to escape from it.

They had, however, no ship, and although all around them tall trees grew, no one of them knew anything of ship building. Still, so strong was their desire to leave the hated spot that they resolved to build one.

They set to work with a will. Soon the sound of saw and hammer awoke the silence of the forest. High and low, noble and peasant, as well as Native people, all worked together.

At length their labors were over, and the rough little ship was afloat. It made but a sorry appearance. The planks were rough-hewn by the hatchet and caulked with the moss which grew in long streamers on the trees. The cordage was Indian-made, and the sails were patched together from shirts and bedclothes. Never before had men thought to dare the ocean waves in so crazy a craft. But the colonists were in such eagerness to be gone, that they chose rather to risk almost certain death upon the ocean than remain longer in their vast prison house.

So they loaded the ship with as much food as they could collect, and saying farewell to their friends, they spread their patchwork sails, and glided out to sea drunken with joy at the thought of returning to France.

At first the wind blew fair, and the little ship sped swiftly homeward. Then came a calm. The sun burned overhead, no faintest breeze stirred the slack sails, and the ship lay as if at anchor upon the glassy waters. And as the ship lay motionless, the slender stock of food grew less and less. Soon there was nothing left but maize, and little of that. At first a tiny handful was each man's daily portion; then it was counted by grains. But jealously hoarded although it was, the maize at length gave out, and there was nothing left to eat but their leather shoes and jerkins.

Then to the pain of hunger was added the pain of thirst, for the water barrels were emptied to the last drop. Unable to endure the torture, some drank the sea water and so died in madness. Beneath the burning sun, every timber of the crazy little ship warped and started, and on all sides the sea flowed in. Still through all their agony, the men clung to life. And sick with hunger, maddened with thirst as they were, they labored unceasingly, bailing out the water. But they labored now with despair in their hearts, and they gave up hope of ever seeing their beloved France again. Then at length the pitiless sun was overcast, a wild wind arose, and the glassy sea, whipped to fury, became a waste of foam and angry billows. The tiny vessel was tossed about helplessly and buffeted this way and that.

"In the turning of a hand," says an old writer, "the waves filled their vessel half full of water, and bruised it upon the one side."

The wretched men now gave themselves up for lost. They cared no longer to bail but cast themselves down into the bottom of the boat, and let it drift where it would. Only one man among them did not utterly lose heart. He set himself now to encourage the others, telling them that if only the wind held, in three days they would see the shores of France.

This man was so full of hope that at length he aroused the others from their despair. Once more they began the weary work of bailing, and in spite of all the fury of the wind and waves, the little vessel kept afloat.

At last the storm passed. Once more the fainting wanderers righted their vessel and turned the prow towards the shores of France. But three days passed, and no land was seen, and they became more despairing than before.

For now the last grain of corn was eaten, the last drop of water drunk. Mad with thirst, sick with hunger, the men strained their weary eyes over the rolling waste of waters. No land was in sight. Then a terrible thought crept into one mind after another. In a low hoarse whisper, one man and then another spoke out his thought - that one man should die for his fellows.

So deep were they sunk in woe that all were of one mind. So lots were cast, and the man upon whom the lot fell was killed.

These tortured wayfarers had become cannibals.

Kept alive in this terrible fashion, the men sailed on, and at length a faint gray streak appeared on the horizon. It was the long-looked-for shore of France. But the joy was too great for their over-strained minds. The sight of land seemed to rob them of all power of thought or action. With salvation in sight, they let the little vessel drift aimlessly this way and that.

While they thus drifted aimlessly, a white sail hove in sight, and an English vessel bore down upon them. In the English vessel there happened to be a Frenchman who had sailed with Ribault on his first voyage to Florida. He soon recognized his countrymen in spite of their sorry plight, and they were brought aboard the English vessel. And when they had been given food and drink, and were somewhat revived, they told their tale of misery.

The Englishmen were in doubt for some time as to what it was best to do. In the end, they decided to set the most feeble on the shores of France, and to carry the others prisoners to the Queen of England, who at that time was about to send an expedition to Florida.

So ended the first attempt of the French to found a colony in North America.

Notes:

Francis I's quote can be found in Picture of Quebec, *by Alfred Hawkins, 1834.*

The description of the May Day landing is from Jean Ribault's letters home.

The Timucua were a large people group that lived in northern Florida and southern Georgia. They spoke dialects of the same language, but the various tribes were not united politically. Their population at the time of the first contact with Europeans is estimated to be between 200,000 and 300,000, but by the end of the 1700's, the last few Timucua assimilated into other tribes. They are now considered extinct.

Quotes by Jean Ribault ("Declare your minds," and the statement regarding Albert de la Pierria) are from Divers Voyages Touching the Discovery of America and the Islands Adjacent *by Richard Hakluyt, 1582.*

The number of men left behind at Charlesfort varies by account, between twenty-six and twenty-nine.

A jerkin is a leather vest.

"In the turning of a hand" is from A Book of American Explorers, *by Thomas Wentworth Higginson, 1877.*

Pronunciation Guide:

Huguenot – HYOO-guh-no or HYOO-guh-not

Ribault – ree-BOE

Timucua, Timucuan – tim-OO-kwa, tim-OO-kwan

Chapter 8

How the French Founded a Colony in Florida

Two years after Ribault's ill-fated expedition, another company of Frenchmen set sail for America. This time René de Laudonnière was captain. He had been with Ribault two years before, and now again he landed on the same spot where Ribault had first landed and set up the arms of France.

As they saw his ship come, the Timucuans ran down to the beach, welcoming him with cries of excitement and joy, and taking him by the hand, the chief led him to the pillar which Jean Ribault had set up. It was wreathed in flowers, and baskets of corn stood before it. For the Timucua looked upon it as an idol and made offerings to it. They kissed it with a great show of reverence and begged the Frenchmen to do the same. "Which we would not deny them," says Laudonnière, who himself tells the story, "to the end we might draw them to be more in friendship with us."

Laudonnière was so delighted with the Timucuans' friendly greeting that he resolved to found his colony among these kindly people. So a little way up the river which Ribault had named the River of May, but which is now the St. John's, he built a fort.

It was late one evening in June when the Frenchmen reached the spot where they intended to build the fort; wearied with their long march through the forest, they lay down upon the ground and were soon fast asleep.

But at daybreak, Laudonnière was astir. He commanded a trumpet to be sounded, and when all the men were aroused and stood together, he bade them give thanks to God for their safe arrival. So standing beneath the waving palms, with the deep blue sky arching overhead, the men sang a psalm of thanksgiving and praise. Then kneeling, they prayed long and earnestly.

The prayer ended, the men arose, and full of happy courage, turned to their work. Everyone took part with right good will. Some brought earth, some cut logs; there was not a man who had not a shovel or hatchet or some tool in his hand. The work went on merrily, and soon above the banks of the river the fort rose, secure and strong, fenced and entrenched on every side. In honor of their King Charles, these new colonists called their fort Caroline, just as Ribault had called his Charlesfort.

But as the Timucuan Chief Saturiwa watched the fort grow, he began to be uneasy. He wondered what these strangers were about, and he feared lest they should mean evil towards him. So he gathered his men together, and one day the Frenchmen looked up from their labors to see the heights above them thick with warriors in their war paint.

At once, the Frenchmen dropped their tools and prepared to defend themselves. But Saturiwa, making signs of peace, and leaving most of his warriors behind him, came down into the camp, followed by a band of twenty musicians who blew ear-piercing blasts upon discordant pipes.

Having reached the camp, Saturiwa squatted on his haunches, showing that he wanted to take counsel with the Frenchmen. Then with many signs and gestures, he told the Frenchmen that his great enemies, the Utinas, were near, and that if the Frenchmen wished to continue in friendship with him, they must promise to help him against these powerful and hated foes.

Laudonnière feared to lose Saturiwa's friendship. And thereupon with signs, helped out now and again with a word or two, a treaty was made between the Timucua and the Frenchmen, Laudonnière promising to help Saturiwa against his enemies, the Utinas. With this treaty Saturiwa was delighted, and he commanded his warriors to help the Frenchmen in building their fort, which they very readily did.

Then, mindful of his promise, as soon as the fort was finished, Laudonnière sent off some of his followers under one of his officers to find out who the Utinas really were of whom Saturiwa spoke with such hate. Guided by the Timucuans, this officer soon came upon the Utinas. But instead of fighting with them he made friends with them, which greatly disgusted his Timucuan guide.

Meanwhile Saturiwa, delighted at the idea of being able to crush his enemies with the Frenchmen's help, had gathered all his fighting men together and made ready for war.

Ten chiefs and five hundred warriors, fearful in war paint and feathers, gathered at the call. Then seeing that Laudonnière was not making any preparations for war, he sent messengers to him.

"Our chief has sent us," they said, "and he would know whether you will stand by your promise to show yourself a friend of his friends, an enemy of his enemies, and go with him to war."

"Tell your chief," replied Laudonnière, "that I am not willing to purchase his friendship with the enmity of another. Notwithstanding I will go with him. But first I must gather food for my garrison, neither are my ships ready. An enterprise such as this needs time. Let your chief abide two months, then if he hold himself ready, I will fulfill my promise to him."

The messenger carried this answer to Saturiwa who, when he heard it, was filled with wrath. He was not, however, to be stayed from war, and he determined to go alone.

With great ceremony, he prepared to set out. In an open space near the river, a huge fire was lit. In a wide circle round this, the warriors gathered. Their faces were fearful with paint, and their hair was decorated with feathers or the heads of wolves and bears and other fierce animals. Beside the fire was placed a large bowl of water, and near it Saturiwa stood erect, while his men squatted at his feet. Standing thus he turned his face, distorted with wrath and hatred, towards the enemy's country. First he muttered to himself, then he cried aloud to his god the Sun. And when he had done this for half an hour, he put his hand into the bowl of water, and sprinkled the heads of his warriors. Then suddenly, as if in anger, he cast the rest of the water into the fire, putting it out. As he did so, he cried aloud:

"So may the blood of our enemies be poured out and their lives extinguished."

In reply, a hoarse yell went up from the Timucuan host, and all the woods resounded with the fierce noise.

Thus Saturiwa and his warriors set forth for battle. In a few days they returned, singing praises to the Sun and bringing with them twenty-four prisoners and many scalps.

And now Laudonnière made Saturiwa more angry than ever with him, for he demanded two of these prisoners. Laudonnière wanted them so that he might send them back to the chief of the Utina as a proof that he at least was still friendly, for he already regretted his treaty with the Timucua. But when Saturiwa heard Laudonnière's request, he was very angry and treated it with scorn.

"Tell your chief," he said, "that he has broken his oath, and I will not give him any of my prisoners."

When Laudonnière heard this answer, he in his turn was very angry, and he resolved to frighten Saturiwa into doing what he wanted. So taking twenty soldiers with him, he went to his village. Leaving some of the soldiers at the gate and charging them to let no Timucuan go in or out, Laudionnère went into Saturiwa's hut with the others. In perfect silence he came in, in perfect silence he sat down and remained so for a long time which, says Laudonnière, put Saturiwa "deeply in his dumps."

At length when he thought that Saturiwa was completely frightened, Laudonnière spoke.

"Where are your prisoners?" he said. "I command them to be brought before me." Thereupon Saturiwa, "angry at the heart and astonished wonderfully," stood a long time without making any answer. But when at last he spoke, it was boldly and without fear.

"I cannot give you my prisoners," he said. "For seeing you coming in such warlike guise, they were afraid and fled to the woods. And not knowing what way they went, we could not by any means find them again."

Laudonnière, however, pretended that he did not understand what Saturiwa said, and again he asked for the prisoners.

Saturiwa then commanded his son to go in search of them, and in about an hour he returned bringing them with him. As soon as they were brought before Laudonnière, the prisoners greeted him humbly. They lifted up their hands to heaven, and then threw themselves at his feet. But Laudonnière raised them at once and led them away to the fort, leaving Saturiwa very angry.

Laudonnière now sent the prisoners back to the Utina's leader, who was greatly delighted at the return of his men. He was still more delighted when the Frenchmen marched with him against another tribe who were his enemies and defeated them.

But while Laudonnière was thus making both friends and enemies among the Native people, all was not peace in the colony itself. Many of the adventurers had grown tired of the loneliness and sameness of the life. The food was bad, the work was hard, and there seemed little hope that things would ever be better. And for all their hardships, it seemed to them the Governor was to blame. So they began to murmur and be discontented, gathering together in groups, whispering that it would be a good deed to put an end to Laudonnière and choose another captain.

And now when the discontent was at its height, Laudonnière fell ill. Then one of the ringleaders of the discontent urged the doctor to put poison in his medicine. But the doctor refused. Next they formed a plot to hide a barrel of gunpowder under his bed and blow him up. But Laudonnière discovered that plot, and the ringleader fled to the forest.

About this time, a ship arrived from France bringing food for the colony, so that for a time, things went a little better. And when the ship sailed again for home, Laudonnière sent the worst of the mutineers back in it. In their place, the captain left behind some of his sailors. But this proved a bad exchange. For these sailors were little better than pirates, and very soon they became the ringleaders in revolt. They persuaded some of the older colonists to join them. And one day, they stole a little ship belonging to the colony and set off on a plundering expedition to the West Indies.

On the seas they led a wild and lawless life, taking and plundering Spanish ships. But after a time, they ran short of food and found themselves forced to put into a Spanish port. Here in order to make peace with the Spaniards, they told all they knew about the French colony.

Thus it was that for the first time the Spaniards learned that the heretic Frenchmen had settled in their land, and speedily the news was sent home to Spain.

Meanwhile, Laudonnière was greatly grieved for the loss of his ship. And as days passed and there was no sign of the mutineers' return, he set his men to work to build two new ships.

For a time, the work went well. But soon many of the men grew tired of it, and they began to grumble. Why should men of noble birth, they asked, slave like carpenters? And day by day, the discontent increased.

At last one Sunday morning, the men sent a message to Laudonnière asking him to come out to the parade ground to meet them. Laudonnière went, and he found all the colony waiting for him with gloomy faces. At once one of them stepped forward and asked leave to read a paper in the name of all the others. Laudonnière gave permission. The paper was read. It was full of complaints about the hard work, the want of food, and other grievances. It ended with a request that the men should be allowed to take the two ships which were being built and sail to Spanish possessions in search of food. In fact, they wanted to become pirates like those mutineers who had already sailed away.

Laudonnière refused to listen to this request. But he promised that as soon as the two ships were finished, they should be allowed to set out in search of gold mines.

The mutineers separated with gloomy faces; they were by no means satisfied with Laudonnière's answer, and the discontent was as deep as ever. Laudonnière now again became very ill, and the malcontents had it all their own way. Soon nearly everyone in the fort was on their side, and they resolved to put an end to Laudonnière's tyranny.

Late one night about twenty men, all armed to the teeth, gathered together and marched to Laudonnière's hut. Arrived there, they beat loudly on the door demanding entrance. But Laudonnière and his few remaining friends knew well what this loud summons meant, and they refused to open the door. The mutineers, however, were not to be easily held back; they forced open the door, wounding one man who tried to hinder them, and in a few minutes, with drawn swords in hand and angry scowls on their faces, they crowded round the sick man's bed. Then holding a gun at his throat, they commanded him to give them leave to set forth for Spanish waters. But the stern old Huguenot knew no fear. Even with the muzzle of the gun against his throat, he refused to listen to the demands of the lawless crew.

His calmness drove them to fury. With terrible threats, and more terrible oaths, they dragged him from his bed. Loading him with fetters, they carried him out of the fort, threw him into a boat, and rowed him out to the ship which lay anchored in the river. All the loyal colonists had by this time been disarmed, and the fort was completely in the hands of the mutineers. Their leader then drew up a paper giving them leave to set forth to Spanish possessions. And this he commanded Laudonnière to sign.

Laudonnière was completely in the power of the mutineers. He was a prisoner and ill, but his spirit was unbroken, and he refused to sign. Then the mutineers sent him a message saying that if he did not sign, they would come on board the ship and cut his throat. So, seeing no help for it, Laudonnière signed.

The mutineers were now greatly delighted at the success of their schemes. They made haste to finish the two little ships which they had been building, and on the 8th of December they set sail. As they went, they flung taunts at those who stayed behind, calling them fools and dolts and other scornful names, and threatening them with all manner of punishments should they refuse them free entrance to the fort on their return.

As soon as the mutineers were gone, Laudonnière's friends rowed out to him, set him free from his fetters, and brought him back to the colony.

They were now but a very small company, but they were at peace with each other, and there was plenty to do. So the weeks went quickly by. They finished the fort and began to build two new ships to take the place of those which the mutineers had stolen. But they never thought of tilling the ground and sowing seed to provide bread for the future. Thus more than three months passed. Then one day an Indian brought the news that a strange ship was in sight. Laudonnière at once sent some men to find out what ship this might be, and whether it was friend or foe.

It proved to be a Spanish vessel which the mutineers had captured, and which was now manned by them. But the mutineers who had sailed away full of pride and insolence now returned in very humble mood. Their buccaneering had not succeeded as they had hoped. They were starving, and instead of boldly demanding entrance and putting in force their haughty threats, they were eager to make terms. But Laudonnière was not sure whether they really came in peace or not. So he sent out a little boat to the mutineers' ship. On the deck of it there was an officer with one or two men only. But below, thirty men, all armed to the teeth, were hidden. Seeing only these one or two men in the boat, the mutineers let her come alongside. But what was their astonishment when armed men suddenly sprang from the bottom of the boat and swarmed over the sides of their vessel. Many of the mutineers were stupid with drink, all of them were weak with hunger, and before they could seize their arms, or make any resistance, they were overpowered and carried ashore.

There a court-martial was held, and four of the ringleaders were condemned to death. But these bold bad men were loath to die.

"Comrades," said one, turning to the loyal soldiers near, "will you stand by and see us die thus shamefully?"

"These," replied Laudonnière sharply, "are no comrades of mutineers and rebels."

All appeals for mercy were in vain. So the men were shot and their bodies hanged on gibbets near the mouth of the river as a lesson to rebels.

After this, there was peace for a time in Fort Caroline. But it soon became peace with misery, for the colony began to starve. The long-expected ship from France did not come. Rich and fertile land spread all around them, but the colonists had neither plowed nor sown it. They trusted to France for all their food. Now for months no ships had come, and their supplies were utterly at an end.

So in ever increasing misery, the days passed. Some crawled about the meadows and forest, digging for roots and gathering herbs. Others haunted the riverbed in search of shellfish. One man even gathered up all the fish bones he could find and ground them to powder to make bread. But all that they scraped together with so much pain and care was hardly enough to keep body and soul together. They grew so thin that their bones started through the skin. Gaunt, hollow-eyed specters, they lay about the fort sunk in misery or dragged themselves a little way into the forest in search of food. Unless help came from France, they knew that they must all soon die a miserable death. And amid all their misery they clung to that last hope, that help would come from France. So, however feeble they were, however faint with hunger, they would crawl in turns to the top of the hill above the fort, straining their dimming eyes seaward. But no sail appeared.

At length they gave up all hope and determined to leave the hated spot. They had the Spanish ship which the mutineers had captured, and another little vessel besides which they had built. But these were not enough to carry them all to France, so gathering all their last energy they began to build another boat. The hope of getting back to France seemed for a time to put a little strength into their famine-stricken bodies. And while they worked, Laudonnière sailed up the river in search of food. But he returned empty-handed. Famishing men cannot work, and soon the colonists began to weary of their labors.

The neighboring Native people were now their enemies. They indeed now and again brought scant supplies of fish to the starving men. But they demanded so much for it, that soon the colonists were bare of everything they had possessed. They bartered the very shirts from their backs for food. And if they complained of the heavy price, the Indians laughed at them.

"If thou makest so great account of thy merchandise," they jeered, "eat it and we will eat our fish."

But summer passed. The grain began to ripen, and although the neighboring people sold it grudgingly, the colony was relieved from utter misery for the time being.

But now fresh troubles arose, for the Frenchmen quarreled with the chief of the Utinas, for whose sake they had already made enemies of Saturiwa and his tribe.

Thinking themselves treated in an unfriendly manner by the Utinas, the Frenchmen seized their chief, and kept him prisoner until the Utinas promised to pay a ransom of large quantities of grain.

The Utinas agreed only because they saw no other means of freeing their chief. They were furiously angry with the Frenchmen and, seething with indignation against them, they refused to pay an ounce of grain until their chief had been set free. And even then they would not bring it to Fort Caroline, but demanded that the Frenchmen to come for it. The Frenchmen went, but they very quickly saw that they were in great danger, for the village swarmed with armed warriors. After a few days, therefore, although only a small portion of the ransom had been paid, the Frenchmen decided to make for home as fast as possible.

It was a hot July morning on which they set off. Each man besides his gun carried a sack of grain, so the progress was slow. They had not gone far beyond the village when the wild war cry was heard. It was immediately followed by a shower of arrows. The Frenchmen replied with a hot fire of bullets. Several of the Utinas fell dead, and the rest fled into the forest.

Then the Frenchmen marched on again. But they had scarcely gone a quarter of a mile when another war cry was heard in front. It was answered from behind, and the Frenchmen knew themselves surrounded. But they stood their ground bravely. Dropping their bags of corn, they seized their guns. A sharp encounter followed, and soon the Utinas fled again into the forest. But again and again they returned to the attack, and the Frenchmen had to fight every yard of the way. At nine o'clock the fight began, and the sun was setting when at length the Utinas gave up the pursuit. When the Frenchmen reached their boats, they counted their losses. Two had been killed and twenty-two injured, some of them so badly that they had to be carried on board the boats. Of all the bags of grain with which they had started out, only two remained. It was a miserable ending to the expedition.

The plight of the colony was now worse than ever. The two sacks of grain were soon consumed; the feeble efforts at building a ship had come to nothing. But rather than stay longer, the colonists resolved to crowd into the two small vessels they had and sail homeward, if only they could gather food enough for the voyage. But where to get that food, none knew.

One day full of troubled, anxious thoughts, Laudonnière climbed the hill and looked seaward. Suddenly he saw something which made his heart beat fast and brought the color to his wasted cheeks. A great ship, its sails gleaming white in the sunlight, was making for the mouth of the river. As he gazed, another and still another ship hove in sight. Thrilling with excitement, Laudonnière sent a messenger down to the fort with all speed to tell the news, and when they heard it, the men who had seemed scarce able to crawl arose and danced for joy. They laughed and wept and cried aloud, till it seemed as if joy had bereft them of their wits.

But soon fear mingled with their joy. There was something not altogether familiar about the cut and rig of the ships. Were they really the long-looked-for ships from France, or did they belong to their deadly and hated enemies, the Spaniards? They were neither one nor the other. That little fleet was English, under command of the famous admiral, John Hawkins, on his return from taking enslaved Africans to the West Indies. To prove that he came with no evil intent toward Laudonnière's men, he landed with many of his officers colorfully clad and wearing no arms. The famine-stricken colonists hailed him with delight, for it seemed to them that he came as a deliverer.

Gravely and kindly, Hawkins listened to the tale of misery, yet he was glad enough when he heard that the Frenchmen had decided to leave Florida, for he wanted to claim it for Queen Elizabeth and England. When, however, he saw the ships in which they meant to sail homewards, he shook his head. "It was not possible," he said, "for so many souls to cross the broad Atlantic in those tiny barks." So he offered to give all the Frenchmen a free passage to France in his own ships. This Laudonnière refused. Then Hawkins offered to lend him, or sell him, one of his ships. Even this kindness, Laudonnière hesitated to accept.

Thereupon there arose a great uproar among the colonists, they crowded round him clamoring to be gone, threatening that if he refused the Englishman's offer, they would accept it and sail without him.

So Laudonnière yielded. He told Hawkins that he would buy the ship he offered, but he had no money. The Englishman, however, was generous. Instead of money he took the cannon and other things now useless to the colonists. He provided them with food enough for the voyage, and seeing many of the men ragged and barefoot, added among other things fifty pairs of shoes.

Then with kindly good wishes, Hawkins said farewell and sailed away, leaving behind him many grateful hearts. As soon as he was gone the Frenchmen began to prepare to depart also. In a few days all was ready, and they only waited for a fair wind in order to set sail. But as they waited, one day, the fort was again thrown into a state of excitement by the appearance of another fleet of ships. Again the question was asked, were they friends or foes, Spaniards or Frenchmen? At length, after hours of sickening suspense, the question was answered, they were Frenchmen under the command of Ribault.

The long-looked-for help had come at last. It had come when it was no longer looked for, when it was indeed unwelcome to many. For the colonists had grown utterly weary of that sunlit cruel land, and they only longed to go home. France, with any amount of tyranny, was to be preferred before the freedom and the misery of Florida.

But to abandon the colony was now impossible, for besides supplies of food, the French ships had brought many new colonists. This time, too, the men had not come alone but had brought their wives and families with them. Soon the fort which had been so silent and mournful was filled with sounds of talk and laughter. Again, the noise of hatchet and hammer resounded through the woods, and the little forsaken corner of the world awoke once more to life.

Notes:

Some portions of this chapter are taken from History of the First Attempt of the French (the Huguenots) to Colonize the Newly Discovered Country of Florida,*"by René Goulaine de Laudonnière, translated by Richard Hakluyt, 1562.*

Laudonnière brought with him the first European artist to arrive in the New World, Jacques LeMoyne. LeMoyne's drawings of the Timucuans, particularly, show life as it was in early Florida and for the Timucuan people. Unfortunately, nearly all his drawings were destroyed; he later recreated some from memory.

H. E. Marshall referred to the enemies of Chief Saturiwa as the Thimagoes, a name later used to refer to a wider group of Timucuans. The Utina people, who had a chief of the same name, were one of the many Timucua tribes, and an enemy of Saturiwa and his tribe. That is the term I have used in this edition of chapter eight.

"So may the blood of our enemies" can be found in Francis Parkman's Works: Pioneers of France in the New World,*"1906-1907.*

Note about John Hawkins:

Along with being an English naval commander, he was also deeply involved in the slave trade. His stop here in 1565 was on his return from his second transatlantic crossing in which he brought hundreds of captured Africans to the West Indies.

Gibbets were a type of gallows.

Pronunciation Guide:

Laudonnière - LOE-duhn-YARE

Saturiwa – sa-chur-EE-wa

Chapter 9

How the Spaniards Drove the French Out of Florida

Scarcely a week had passed before the new peace and happiness of the French colony was brought to a cruel end.

Late one night, the men on board the French ships saw a great black hulk loom silently up out of the darkness. It was followed by another and another. No word was spoken, and in eerie silence the strange ships crept stealthily onwards and cast anchor beside the French. The stillness grew terrible. At length it was broken by a trumpet call from the deck of one of the silent newcomers.

Then a voice came through the darkness. "Gentlemen," it asked, "whence does this fleet come?"

"From France," was the reply.

"What are you doing here?" was the next question.

"We are bringing soldiers and supplies for a fort which the King of France has in this country, and for many which he soon will have."

"Are you Catholics or Lutherans?"

The question came sharply across the dark water. It was answered by many voices.

"We are Lutherans," cried the French. "We are of the new religion."

Then it was the Frenchmen's turn to ask questions.

"Who are you," they cried, "and whence come ye?"

"I am Pedro Menendez," replied the voice out of the darkness. "I am Admiral of the fleet of the King of Spain. And I am come into this country to hang and behead all Lutherans whom I may find by land or by sea. And my King has given me such strict commands that I have power to pardon no man of them. And those commands I shall obey to the letter, as you will see. At dawn I shall come aboard your ship. And if there I find any Catholic he shall be well-treated, but every heretic shall die."

In reply to this speech a shout of wrath went up from the Frenchmen.

"If you are a brave man," they cried, "why wait for dawn? Come on now, and see what you will get."

Then in their anger, they heaped insults upon the Spaniards and poured forth torrents of scoffing words. Thereupon Menendez was so enraged that he swore to silence those "Lutheran dogs" once and forever. So the order was given, and his great ship slowly moved towards the French.

The threats of the French had been but idle boasting; they could not withstand the Spaniards, for their leader was ashore with most of his soldiers. So cutting their cables, they fled out to sea pursued by the foe.

There was a mad chase through the darkness. But the heretic devils, as the Spaniards called them, were skillful sailors. Menendez could not catch them, and when day dawned he gave up the chase and moodily turned back to Fort Caroline.

Here he found the French ready for him, and they seemed so strong that he would not attack, but sailed away southwards until he reached the river of Dolphins.

Here Menendez landed and took possession of the country in the name of the King of Spain. While cannon boomed and trumpets blew, he stepped on shore, followed by his officers and gentlemen. In all the trappings of knighthood, with many-colored banners fluttering in the breeze, they marched. Then as they advanced, another procession came toward them. At the head of it was a priest in all the pomp and splendor of his priestly robes. He carried a gilded crucifix in his hand, and as he marched he sang a Te Deum.

When the two processions met, Menendez and all his company knelt, and baring their heads, kissed the crucifix. So was the land claimed for Spain and the Catholic faith, and St. Augustine, the oldest town in the United States, was founded.

Meanwhile, the fleeing French ships had turned, followed the Spaniards, and seen them land. Then they went back to Fort Caroline with the news.

While these things had been happening, Laudonnière had been very ill. He was still in bed when Ribault, followed by several of his chief officers, came to his room to tell him the news which the returning ships had just brought. And beside his sickbed, they held a council of war. It was decided to attack the Spaniards and drive them from the land. But how?

First one plan and then another was discussed, and to each someone objected. But at length it was decided to go by sea and attack the Spaniards suddenly in their newly-founded fort.

So almost every man who could hold a gun set forth with Ribault, and Laudonnière was left in the fort with the feeble and sick, and scarcely a man besides who had ever drawn a sword or fired a shot. Their leader was as sick and feeble as any of them. But he dragged himself from his bed to review his forces. They were poor indeed, but Laudonnière made the best of them. He appointed each man to a certain duty, he set a watch night and day, and he began to repair the broken-down walls of the fort, so that they would be able to make some show of resistance in case of attack.

While Laudonnière was thus ordering his poor little garrison, the ships carrying the rest of the colonists sailed on their way. The wind was fair, and in the night they crept close to where the Spanish vessels lay.

But when day dawned and the Spaniards saw the French vessels close to them, they fled to the shelter of their harbor. And a sudden storm arising, the French were driven out to sea again.

As Menendez watched them from the shore, he rejoiced. He knew by the number of the ships that most of the French colonists must be in them, and he hoped that they would all be lost in the storm.

Then as he watched, a sudden thought came to him. While the Frenchmen were battling with wind and waves, he resolved to move quickly over land and take Fort Caroline. For he knew that it must be almost, if not quite, unprotected.

One of the French mutineers who had deserted Laudonnière was now in the Spanish fort. He would show the way. Full of this splendid idea, eager to carry it out at once, he ordered Mass to be said, then he called a council and laid his plan before his officers. They, however, met his eagerness with coldness. It was a mad and hopeless plan, they thought, and they did their best to dissuade Menendez from it. But Menendez was determined to go.

"Comrades," he said, "it is now that we must show our courage and our zeal. This is God's war, and we must not turn our backs upon it. It is war against heretics, and we must wage it with blood and with fire."

But the Spanish leader's eager words awoke no response in the hearts of his hearers. They answered him only with mutterings. Still Menendez insisted. The debate grew stormy, and angry words were flung this way and that.

At length, however, Menendez had his way. The clamor was stilled, the officers gave a grudging consent, and preparations for the march were begun. In a few days all was ready, and the expedition set out. It was a simple matter. There was no great train of sumpter mules or baggage wagons. Each man carried his own food and ammunition, and twenty axmen marched in front of the little army to cleave a way through the forest.

The storm still raged. Rain fell in torrents, and the wind howled ceaselessly as on and on the men trudged. They plunged through seas of mud, and grass which grew waist high, and threaded their way along the narrow paths cloven for them by the axmen.

So for three days they toiled onward. Their food was gone, their ammunition soaked, they were drenched to the skin, footsore and famishing, when upon the third night they lay down upon the muddy ground, cursing their leader for having brought them forth to die so miserably. But while the men cursed, Menendez prayed. All night he prayed. And before day dawned, he called his officers to a council. They were now within a mile of Fort Caroline, and he was eager to attack.

But his officers were sick of the whole business. The men were utterly disheartened; one and all they clamored to return.

Yet once again Menendez bent them to his will. In the darkness of the forest, he spoke to the wretched, shivering, rain-drenched men. He taunted, he persuaded, and at length wrung from them a sullen consent to follow him.

So once again the miserable march was begun, and when day dawned, they stood on the hill above the fort.

No sound came from it, no watchman stood upon the ramparts. For towards morning, seeing that it rained harder than ever, the captain of the guard had sent his men to bed, for they were soaked to the skin and he was sorry for them. In such rain and wind what enemy would venture forth? he asked himself. It was folly to stay abroad on such a night, he thought. So he dismissed the guard and went off to bed.

Thus none heard or saw the approach of the Spaniards. Then suddenly the silence of the dawn was broken with fierce war cries.

"At them," shouted the Spaniards. "God is with us!"

The sleeping Frenchmen started from their beds in terror. Half-naked, they sprang to arms. On every side the Spaniards poured in. The dim light of dawn showed the cruel faces and the gleam of drawn swords. Then clash of steel, screams of frightened women and children, curses, prayers, all mingled together in terrible confusion.

At the first alarm, Laudonnière sprang from his bed, and seizing his sword called his men to follow him. But the Spaniards surrounded him, his men were slain and scattered, and he himself was forced back into the yard of his house. Here there was a tent. This stopped his pursuers, for they stumbled over the cordage and became entangled with it. The confusion gave Laudonnière a few minutes' respite in which he escaped through a breach in the ramparts and took refuge in the forest. A few others fleeing this way and that escaped likewise. But some, the first moment of terror past, resolved to return and throw themselves on the mercy of the Spaniards rather than face starvation in the woods.

"They are men," said one. "It may be when their fury is spent, they will spare our lives. Even if they slay us, what of that? It is but a moment's pain. Better that than to starve here in the woods or be torn to pieces by wild beasts."

Still some held back, but most agreed to throw themselves upon the mercy of the Spaniards.

So unarmed and almost naked as they were, they turned back to give themselves up. But little did these simple Frenchmen understand the fury of the foe. When they neared the fort, the Spaniards rushed out upon them and, unheeding their cries for mercy, slew them to a man. Those who had held back, when they saw the fate of their companions, fled through the forest. Some sought refuge among the Native people. But even from that refuge the Spaniards hunted them forth and slew them without pity. Thus the land was filled with blood-shed and ruin. Many were slain at once by the sword, others were hanged on trees round the fort, and over them Menendez wrote, "I do not this not as unto Frenchmen but as unto Lutherans." Only a few miserable stragglers, after untold sufferings, reached the little ship which still lay at anchor in the river. Among these was Laudonnière.

Their one desire now was to flee homewards, and unfurling their sails, they set out for France.

The colony of Fort Caroline was wiped out, and rejoicing at the success of his bold scheme, Menendez marched back to St. Augustine where a Te Deum was sung in honor of this victory over heretics.

Meanwhile the Frenchmen who had set forth to attack St. Augustine by sea had been driven hither and thither by the storm, and at length were wrecked. But although the ships were lost, all, or nearly all, of the men succeeded in reaching the shore in safety. And not knowing what had happened at Fort Caroline, they set out in two companies to try to reach the fort by land.

But they never reached the fort. For one morning scarcely ten days after the destruction of Fort Caroline, some Native people came to Menendez with the news that they had seen a French ship wrecked a little to the south.

The news delighted Menendez, and he at once set out to capture the shipwrecked men. It was not long before he saw the lights of the French camp in the distance. But on coming nearer it was seen that they were on the other side of an arm of the sea, so that it was impossible to reach them. Hiding, therefore, in the bushes by the water's edge, Menendez and his men watched the Frenchmen on the other side. The Spaniards soon saw that their enemies were in distress.

They suspected that they were starving, for they could be seen walking up and down the shore seeking shellfish. But Menendez wanted to make sure of the state they were in, and he made up his mind to get nearer to the Frenchmen. So he put off his fine clothes, and dressing himself like a common sailor, got into a boat and rowed across the water.

Seeing him come, one of the Frenchmen swam out to meet him. As he drew near, Menendez called out to him: "Who are you, and whence come ye?"

"We are followers of Ribault, Viceroy of the King of France," answered the Frenchman.

"Are you Catholics or Lutherans?" asked Menendez.

"We are Lutherans," answered the man.

Then after a little more talk, Menendez told who he was.

With this news, the man swam back to his companions. But he soon returned to the boat to say that five of the French leaders wished to speak with the Spanish leader, and begged for safe conduct to his camp.

To this Menendez readily agreed, and returning to his own side, he sent the boat back to bring the Frenchmen over.

When they landed, Menendez received them courteously. And after returning his ceremonious greetings, the Frenchmen begged the Spaniards to lend them a boat so that they might cross the river which lay between them and Fort Caroline.

At this request, Menendez smiled evilly. "Gentlemen," he said, "it were idle for you to go to your fort. It has been taken, and every man is slain."

But the Frenchmen could not at first believe that he spoke the truth. So in proof of his words, the Spanish leader bade his men show the heretics the plunder which had been taken from their fort. As they looked upon it, the hearts of the Frenchmen sank.

Then ordering breakfast to be sent to them, Menendez left them and went to breakfast with his own officers.

Breakfast over, he came back to the Frenchmen, and as he looked at their gloomy faces, his heart rejoiced. "Do you believe now," he asked, "that what I told you is true?"

"Yes," replied the Frenchmen. "We believe. It would be useless now to go to the fort. All we ask of you is to lend us ships so that we may return home."

"I would gladly do so," replied Menendez, "if you were Catholics, and if I had ships. But I have none."

Then seeing that he would give them no help to reach home, the Frenchmen begged Menendez at least to let them stay with his people until help came to them from France. It was little enough to ask, they thought, as France and Spain were at peace. But there was no pity or kindliness in the Spanish general's heart.

"All Catholics," he replied sternly, "I would defend and succour. But as for you, you are Lutherans, and I must hold you as enemies. I will wage war against you with blood and fire. I will wage it fiercely, both by land and sea, for I am Viceroy for my King in this country. I am here to plant the holy Gospel in this land, that the Indians may come to the light and knowledge of the Holy Catholic, faith of our Lord Jesus Christ, as taught by the Roman Church. Give up your banners and your arms, and throw yourselves on my mercy, and I will do with you as God gives me grace. In no other way can you have truce or friendship with me."

To this the Frenchmen knew not what to say. First they consulted together, then some of them went back across the water to take counsel with those who waited there. They talked long, and anxiously those on the Spanish side awaited their return. At length one of their messengers returned, and going to Menendez he offered him a large sum of money if he would swear to spare their lives.

But Menendez would promise nothing. The Frenchmen were helpless. They were starving and in his hands. And both he and they knew it. They saw no hope anywhere, so they yielded to the Spanish general's demands.

Once more the boat was sent across the water, and this time it came back laden with banners, arms, and armor. Then guarded by Spanish soldiers, the Frenchmen were brought across by tens. As each batch landed, they found themselves prisoners; their arms were taken from them, and their hands were tied behind their backs.

All day, hour after hour, the boat plied to and fro: and when all the Frenchmen had been brought over, they were ordered to march forward. The Spanish general walked in front. But he did not go far, for the sun was already setting, and it was time to camp for the night. So but a little way from the shore he stopped, and drew a line in the sand. And when the wretched Frenchmen reached that line, weaponless and helpless as they were, they were one and all put to death. Then, glorying in his deed, Menendez returned to St. Augustine.

But he had not yet completely wiped out the French colony. For besides those he had so ruthlessly slain, there was another large party under Ribault, who, ignorant of all that had happened, were still slowly making their way to Fort Caroline. But again news of their whereabouts was brought to Menendez by the Native people, and again he set off to waylay them.

He found them on the same spot as he had found the first party. But this time the Frenchmen had made a raft, and upon this they were preparing to cross the water when the Spaniards came upon them. The Frenchmen were in such misery that many of them greeted the appearance of their enemies with joy. But others were filled with misgiving. Still they resolved to try to make terms with the Spaniards. So first one of his officers, and then Ribault himself, rowed across the strip of water to parley with the Spanish leader. They found him as pitiless as their companions had found him. And seeing that they could make no terms with him, many of the Frenchmen refused to give themselves up, and they marched away. But after much parleying and many comings and goings across the river, Ribault, believing that Menendez would spare their lives, yielded up himself and the rest of his company to the Spaniards.

He was soon undeceived, for he was led away among the bushes, and his hands were tied behind his back. As his followers came over they, too, were bound and led away. Then as trumpets blew and drums beat, the Spaniards fell upon their helpless prisoners and slew them to a man.

When Ribault saw that his hour was come, he did not flinch. "We are but dust," he said, "and to dust we must return: twenty years more or less can matter little." So with the words of a psalm upon his lips he met the sword-thrust.

Not till every man lay dead was the fury of the Spaniards sated. Then, his horrible labor ended, Menendez returned once more in triumph to his fort.

Those of the French who had refused to give themselves up to Menendez now wandered back to the shore where their ship had been wrecked. Out of the broken pieces, they tried to build a ship in which they might sail homeward. But again news of their doings was brought to Menendez by the Native people. And again he set out to crush them. When the Frenchmen saw the Spaniards come, they fled in terror. But Menendez sent a messenger after them, promising that if they yielded to him he would spare their lives. Most of them yielded. And Menendez kept his promise. He treated his prisoners well. But, when an opportunity arrived, he sent them home to end their lives as galley slaves.

Notes:

Some passages are from History of the First Attempt of the French (the Huguenots) to Colonize the Newly Discovered Country of Florida, *by René Goulaine de Laudonnière, translated by Richard Hakluyt, 1562.*

Sumpter mules are beasts of burden, which carry materials on their backs rather than pulling them.

From the time of the massacre in Florida, the inlet has been called "Matanzas," for the Spanish word for "slaughters."

Chapter 10

How a Frenchman Avenged the Death of His Countrymen

When the news of these terrible massacres reached France, it was greeted with a cry of horror. Even the boy King, Charles IX, Catholic though he was, demanded redress. But the King of Spain declared that the Frenchmen had been justly served. The land upon which they had settled was his, he said, and they had no right to be there. He was sorry that they were Frenchmen, but they were also pirates and robbers, and had received only the just reward of their misdeeds.

Neither Charles nor his mother Catherine de Medici, who was the real ruler in France at this time, wished to quarrel with the King of Spain. So finding that no persuasions would move him, and that instead of being punished Menendez was praised and rewarded, they let the matter drop.

But there was one man in France who would not thus tamely submit to the tyranny of Spain. His name was Dominique de Gourgues, a Catholic. He hated the Spaniards with a deadly hatred. And when he heard of the Florida massacre, he vowed to avenge the death of his Protestant countrymen. He sold all that he had, borrowed what money he could, and with three ships and a goodly company of soldiers and sailors, set sail.

At first, however, he kept his real object secret. Instead of steering straight for Florida, he steered southward, saying that he was going to Africa for slaves. But after encountering storms and contrary winds he turned westward, and when off the coast of Cuba, he gathered all his men together and told them what he had set out to do.

In vivid, terrible words he recounted to them the horrible slaughter. "Shall we let such cruelty go unpunished?" he asked. "What fame for us if we avenge it! To this end I have given my fortune, and I counted on you to help me. Was I wrong?"

"No," they all cried. "We will go with you to avenge our countrymen!"

So with hearts filled with thoughts of vengeance, they sailed onward to Fort Caroline.

The Spaniards had repaired the fort and now called it Fort Mateo. They had also built two small forts nearer the mouth of the river to guard the entrance to it. Now one afternoon, the men in these forts saw three ships go sailing by. These were the French ships bringing Gourgues and his companions. But the men in the forts thought that they were Spanish ships and therefore fired a salute. Gourgues did not undeceive them. He fired a salute in reply and, sailing on as if he were going elsewhere, was soon lost to sight.

At length, having found a convenient place out of sight of the forts, he drew to the shore. But when he would have landed, he saw that the whole beach was crowded with Native people, armed with bows and arrows and ready for war. For the Timucua, too, had taken the strange ships to be Spanish. And as they had grown to hate the Spaniards with a deadly hatred, they were prepared to withstand their landing.

Fortunately, however, Gourges had on board a trumpeter who had been in Florida with Laudonnière. So now he sent him on shore to talk with the Timucua. And as soon as they recognized him, they greeted him with shouts of joy. Then they led him at once to their chief, who was no other than Saturiwa, Laudonnière's one-time friend.

So amid great rejoicings, the Frenchmen landed. Then Saturiwa poured into their ears the tale of his wrongs. He told them how the Spaniards stole their corn, drove them from their huts and their hunting grounds, and generally ill-treated them. "Not one peaceful day," he said, "have the Indians known since the Frenchmen went away."

When Gourgues heard this, he was well-pleased. "If you have been ill-treated by the Spaniards," he said, "the French will avenge you."

At this, Saturiwa leaped for joy.

"What!" he cried. "Will you fight the Spaniards?"

"Yes," replied Gourgues, "but you must do your part also."

"We will die with you," cried Saturiwa, "if need be."

"That is well," said Gourgues. "How soon can you be ready? For if we fight, we should fight at once."

"In three days we can be ready," said the leader.

"See to it then," said Gourgues, "that you are secret in the matter so that the Spaniards suspect nothing."

"Have no fear," replied Saturiwa. "We wish them more ill than you do."

The third day came and, true to his word, Saturiwa appeared, surrounded by hundreds of warriors, fearful in paint and feathers. Then some by water, some by land, the French and Timucua set forth, and after many hardships and much toil, they reached one of the forts which the Spaniards had built near the river's mouth. From the shelter of the surrounding trees, they gazed upon it.

"There!" cried Gourgues. "There at last are the thieves who have stolen this land from our King. There are the murderers who slew our countrymen."

At his words, the men were hardly to be restrained. In eager whispers, they begged to be led on. So the word was given, and the Frenchmen rushed upon the fort.

The Spaniards had just finished their midday meal when a cry was heard from the ramparts. "To arms! To arms! The French are coming!"

They were taken quite unawares, and with but short resistance they fled. The French and Timucua pursued them and hemmed them in so that not one man escaped. In like manner the second fort was also taken, and every man slain or made prisoner.

The next day was Sunday, and Gourgues spent it resting and making preparations to attack Fort Mateo.

When the Spaniards in Fort Mateo saw the French and their great host of yelling, dancing Timucua, they were filled with fear. And in order to find out how strong the force really was, one of them dressed himself as a Timucuan and crept within the French lines. But almost at once he was seen by a young Timucua chief. And his disguise being thus discovered, he was seized and questioned. He owned that there were scarce three hundred men in the fort and that, believing the French to number at least two thousand, they were completely terror-stricken. This news delighted Gourgues, and next morning he prepared to attack.

The fort was easily taken. When the Spaniards saw the French attack, panic seized them, and they fled into the forest. But there the Timucua, mad with the desire of blood and vengeance, met them. Many fell before the tomahawks; others turned back, choosing rather to die at the hands of the French than of the Timucua. But which way they turned, there was no escape. Nearly all were slain, a few only were taken prisoner.

When the fight was over, Gourgues brought all the prisoners from the three forts together. He led them to the trees where Menendez had hanged the Frenchmen a few months before. There he spoke to them.

"Did you think that such foul treachery, such abominable cruelty would go unpunished?" he said. "Nay, I, one of the most lowly of my King's subjects, have taken upon myself to avenge it. There is no name shameful enough with which to brand your deeds, no punishment severe enough to repay them. But though you cannot be made to suffer as you deserve, you shall suffer all that an enemy may honorably inflict. Thus your fate shall be an example to teach others to keep the peace and friendly alliance, which you have broken so wickedly."

And having spoken thus sternly to the trembling wretches, Gourgues ordered his men to hang them on the very same trees upon which Menendez had hanged the Frenchmen. And over their heads he nailed tablets of wood upon which were burned the words, "I do not this as unto Spaniards nor as unto Mariners, but as unto Traitors, Robbers and Murderers."

Then at length, the vengeance of Gourgues was satisfied. But indeed it was scarce complete, for Menendez, the leader of the Spaniards was safe in Europe, and beyond the reach of any private man's vengeance. The Spaniards, too, were strongly entrenched at St. Augustine, so strongly indeed that Gourgues knew he had not force enough to oust them. He had not even men enough to keep the three forts he had won. So he resolved to destroy them.

This delighted the Timucua, and they worked with such vigor that in one day, all three forts were made level with the ground. Then, having accomplished all that he had come to do, Gourgues made ready to depart. Whereupon the Timucua set up a wail of grief. With tears they begged the Frenchmen to stay, and when they refused, they followed them all the way to the shore, praising them and giving them gifts, and praying them to return.

So leaving the people weeping upon the shore, the Frenchmen sailed away, and little more than a month later they reached home.

When they heard of what Gourgues had done, the Huguenots rejoiced, and they greeted him with honor and praise. But Philip of Spain was furiously angry. He demanded that Gourgues should be punished, and offered a large sum of money for his head. King Charles, too, being in fear of the King of Spain, looked upon him coldly, so that for a time he was obliged to flee away and hide himself.

Gourgues had used all his money to set forth on his expedition, so for a few years he lived in poverty. But Queen Elizabeth at length heard of him and his deeds. And as she, too, hated the Spaniards, she was pleased at what he had done, and she asked him to enter her service. Thus at length, he was restored to honor and favor. And in honor and favor he continued all the rest of his life.

Notes:

Some of this chapter is taken from Historical collections of Louisiana and Florida, including translations of original manuscripts relating to their discovery and settlement, with numerous historical and biographical notes, *by B. F. French, A. Mason, first published in 1869, J. Sabin & Sons.*

The inscription on tablets of wood is from History of the First Attempt of the French (the Huguenots) to Colonize the Newly Discovered Country of Florida, *by René Goulaine de Laudonnière, translated by Richard Hakluyt, 1562.*

Pronunciation Guide:
Dominique de Gourgues – doe-mee-NEEK duh GORG

Chapter 11

The Adventures of Sir Humphrey Gilbert

The terrible disasters in Florida did not altogether stop French adventurers from going to the New World. But to avoid conflict with Spain, they sailed henceforth more to the northern shores of America and endeavored to found colonies there. This made Englishmen angry. For by right of Cabot's voyages, they claimed all America from Florida to Newfoundland, which, says a writer in the time of Queen Elizabeth, "they brought and annexed unto the crowne of England." The English, therefore, looked upon the French as interlopers and usurpers. The French, however, paid little attention to the English claims. They explored the country, named mountains, rivers, capes, and bays, and planted colonies where they liked. Thus began the long two hundred years' struggle between the French and English for possession of North America.

The French had already planted a colony on the St. Lawrence River when an Englishman, Sir Humphrey Gilbert, determined also to plant one in North America.

He was the first Englishman ever to attempt to found a colony in America. Many Englishmen had indeed sailed there before him. But they had only gone in quest of gold and of adventures, and without any thought of founding a New England across the seas. This now, with Queen Elizabeth's permission, was what Sir Humphrey hoped to do.

He set out with a little fleet of five ships. One of these was called the *Raleigh*, and it had been fitted out by the famous Sir Walter Raleigh, who was Gilbert's stepbrother. Walter Raleigh, no doubt, would gladly have gone with the company himself. But he was at the time in high favor with Good Queen Bess, and she forbade him to go on any such dangerous expedition. So he had to content himself with helping to fit out expeditions for other people.

The *Raleigh* was the largest ship of the little fleet, and Sir Walter spared no cost in fitting it out. But before they had been two days at sea, the Captain of the *Raleigh* and many of his men fell ill. This so greatly discouraged them that they turned back to Plymouth.

Sir Humphrey was sad indeed at the loss of the largest and best-fitted ship of his expedition, but he held on his way undaunted. They had a troublous passage. Contrary winds, fogs, and icebergs delayed them. In a fog, two of the ships named the *Swallow* and the *Squirrel* separated from the others. But still Sir Humphrey sailed on.

At length, land came in sight. But it was a barren, unfriendly coast, "nothing appearing unto us but hideous rocks and mountains, bare of trees, and void of any green herb," says one who went with the expedition. And seeing it so uninviting, they sailed southward along the coast, looking for a fairer land.

And now to their great joy, they fell in again with the *Swallow*. The men in the *Swallow* were glad, too, to see the *Golden Hind* and the *Delight* once more. They threw their caps into the air and shouted aloud for joy.

Soon after the reappearance of the *Swallow*, the *Squirrel* also turned up, so the four ships were together again. Together they sailed into the harbor of St. John's in Newfoundland. Here they found fishermen from all countries. For Newfoundland had by this time become famous as a fishing-ground, and every summer, ships from all countries went there to fish.

Sir Humphrey, armed as he was with a commission from Queen Elizabeth, was received with all honor and courtesy by these people. And on Monday, August 5, 1583, he landed and solemnly took possession of the country for two hundred leagues north, south, east and west, in the name of England's Queen.

First his commission was read aloud and interpreted to the fishermen of foreign lands who were there. Then one of Sir Humphrey's followers brought him a twig of a hazel tree and a sod of earth and put them into his hands, as a sign that he took possession of the land and all that was in it. Then proclamation was made that these lands belonged to her Majesty Queen Elizabeth of England by the Grace of God, for religion and for loyalty to the Queen. "If any person should utter words sounding to the dishonour of her Majesty," Sir Humphrey told his listeners, "he should lose his ears, and have his ship and goods confiscate." The arms of England, engraved on lead and fixed to a pillar of wood, were then set up, and after prayer to God, the ceremony came to an end. Thus Newfoundland became an English possession, and by right of Sir Humphrey Gilbert's claims, it became the oldest colony of the British Empire.

Sir Humphrey Gilbert had taken possession of the land. But it soon became plain that it would be impossible to found a colony with the wild riffraff of the sea, of which his company was formed. Troubles began at once. A few indeed went about their business quietly, but others spent their time in plotting mischief. They had no desire to stay in that far country; so some hid in the woods waiting a chance to steal away in one or other of the ships which were daily sailing homeward laden with fish. Others more bold plotted to steal one of Sir Humphrey's ships and sail home without him. But their plot was discovered. They, however, succeeded in stealing a ship belonging to some other adventurers. It was laden with fish and ready to depart homeward. In this they sailed away, leaving its owners behind.

The rest of Sir Humphrey's men now clamored more than ever to be taken home. And at length, he yielded to them. But the company was now much smaller than when he set out. For besides those who had stolen away, many had died and many more were sick. There were not enough men to man all four ships. So the *Swallow* was left with the sick and a few colonists who wished to remain, and in the other three Sir Humphrey put to sea with the rest of his company.

He did not, however, sail straight homeward. For he wanted to explore still further, and find, if he could, an island to the south which he had heard was very fertile. But the weather was stormy, and before they had gone far the *Delight* was wrecked, and nearly all on board were lost.

"This was a heavy and grievous event, to lose at one blow our chief ship freighted with great provision, gathered together with much travail, care, long time, and difficulty; but more was the loss of our men, which perished to the number almost of a hundred souls." So wrote Master Edward Hayes who commanded the *Golden Hind*, and who afterwards wrote the story of the expedition.

After this "heavy chance," the two ships that remained beat up and down tacking with the wind, Sir Humphrey hoping always that the weather would clear up and allow him once more to get near land. But day by day passed. The wind and waves continued as stormy as ever, and no glimpse of land did the weary sailors catch.

It was bitterly cold, food was growing scarce, and day by day the men lost courage. At length they prayed Sir Humphrey to leave his search and return homeward. Sir Humphrey had no wish to go, but seeing his men shivering and hungry, he felt sorry for them, and resolved to do as they wished.

"Be content," he said. "We have seen enough, and take no care of expense past: I will set you forth royally the next spring, if God send us safe home."

So the course was changed, and the ships turned eastward. "The wind was large for England at our return," says Hayes, "but very high, and the sea rough." It was so rough that the *Squirrel* in which Sir Humphrey sailed was almost swallowed up. For the *Squirrel* was only a tiny frigate of ten tons. And seeing it battered to and fro, and in danger of sinking every moment, the captain of the *Golden Hind* and many others prayed Sir Humphrey to leave it and come aboard their boat. But Sir Humphrey would not.

"I will not forsake my little company going homeward," he said, "with whom I have passed through many storms and perils."

No persuasions could move him, so the captain of the *Golden Hind* was fain to let him have his way. One afternoon in September, those in the *Golden Hind* watched the little *Squirrel* anxiously as it tossed up and down among the waves. But Sir Humphrey seemed not a whit disturbed. He sat in the stern, calmly reading. And seeing the anxious faces of his friends, he cheerfully waved his hand to them.

"We are as near to heaven by sea as by land," he called, through the roar of waves.

Then the sun went down. Darkness fell over the wild sea, and the ships could only know each other's whereabouts by the tossing lights.

Suddenly to the men on the *Golden Hind* it seemed as if the lights of the little frigate went out. Immediately the watch cried out that the frigate was lost.

It was "too true. For in that moment, the frigate was devoured and swallowed up of the sea."

Yet the men on the *Golden Hind* would not give up hope. All that night they kept watch, straining their eyes through the stormy darkness in the hope of catching sight of the frigate or of some of its crew. But morning came and there was no sign of it on all the wide waste of waters. Still they hoped, and all the way to England they hailed every small sail which came in sight, trusting still that it might be the *Squirrel*. But it never appeared. Of the five ships which set forth, only the *Golden Hind* returned to tell the tale. And thus ended the first attempt to found an English colony in the New World.

Notes:

The account and quotes in this chapter are from Sir Humphrey Gilbert's Voyage to Newfoundland, *by Edward Hayes, 1583. Hayes' story can be found in its entirety in "Voyages and Discoveries," by Richard Hakluyt, Penguin Books, New York, NY: 1972, chapter 43.*

Chapter 12

About Sir Walter Raleigh's Adventures in the Golden West

The first attempt to found an English colony in America had been an utter failure. But the idea of founding a New England across the seas had now taken hold of Sir Humphrey's young step-brother, Walter Raleigh. And a few months after the return of the *Golden Hind*, he received from the Queen a charter very much the same as his brother's. But although he got the charter, Raleigh himself could not sail to America, for Queen Elizabeth would not let him go. So again he had to content himself with sending other people.

It was on April 27, 1584, that his expedition set out in two small ships. Raleigh knew some of the great Frenchmen of the day and had heard of their attempt to found a colony in Florida. And in spite of the terrible fate of the Frenchmen, he thought Florida would be an excellent place to found an English colony.

So Raleigh's ships made their way to Florida and landed on Roanoke Island, off the coast of what is now North Carolina. In those days, of course, there was no Carolina, and the Spaniards called the whole coast Florida, right up to the shores of Newfoundland.

The Englishmen were delighted with Roanoke. It seemed to them a fertile, pleasant land, where the soil was "the most plentiful, sweete, fruitfull and wholsome of all the worlde," Captain Arthur Barlowe wrote to Raleigh. So they at once took possession of it "in the right of the Queen's most excellent Majesty as rightful Queen, and Princess of the same."

Captain Barlowe also wrote that they "found the people most gentle, loving, and faithfull, voide of all guile and treason, and such as live after the manner of the golden age." But the newcomers and the inhabitants found it difficult to understand each other.

"What do you call this country?" asked an Englishman.

"Win gan da coa," answered the people.

So the Englishmen went home to tell of the wonderful country of Wingandacoe. But what the people had really said was, "What fine clothes you have!"

However, the mistake did not matter much to the Englishmen. For they now changed the name of the land from whatever it had been to Virginia, in honor of their Virgin Queen.

This first expedition to Roanoke was only for exploring, and after a couple months, the adventurers sailed home again to tell of all that they had seen. They took with them two Croatoan leaders, whose names were Wanchese and Manteo. When they arrived in England, Manteo taught the Carolina Algonquian language to the scientist Thomas Harriot, and as they prepared for the next voyage, he told him all about life in the New World.

Raleigh was so pleased with the report of Roanoke Island which they brought home to him, that he at once began to make plans for founding a colony there. And the following April, his seven ships were ready, and the expedition of about six hundred men, including Wanchese, Manteo, Harriot, and the artist John White, set out again from Plymouth under his cousin, Sir Richard Grenville.

Sir Richard's ship ran aground on a sand bank near Ocracoke, and most of their food supply was ruined. And now almost as soon as they landed, troubles began between the Englishmen and the Native people. Sir Richard accused a member of the Aquascogoc tribe of stealing a silver cup. When it was not returned as promised, Sir Richard retaliated in rage by setting their entire village and its crops on fire. This was a bad beginning.

Nevertheless, Sir Richard left a colony of over a hundred men in the country. And promising to return with fresh supplies in the following spring, he sailed homeward.

The Governor of this colony was named Ralph Lane. He was wise and able, but he was soon beset with difficulties. He found that the place chosen for a colony was not a good one. For the harbor was bad, the coast dangerous, and Sir Richard's harsh act left many of the Native people angered. So he set about exploring the country, and decided as soon as fresh supplies came from England, he would move to a better spot.

Spring came and passed, and no ships from England appeared. The men began to starve. And seeing this, the people who had feared them before, now began to be scornful and taunt them.

"Your God is not a true god," they said, "or he would not leave you to starve."

They refused to sell the colonists food no matter what price was offered. The conflict with the English was so great indeed that they resolved to sow no corn in order that there should be no harvest, being ready to suffer hunger themselves if they might destroy the colony utterly.

As the days passed, the Englishmen daily felt the pinch of hunger more and more. Then Lane divided his company into three and sent each in a different direction so that they might gather roots and herbs and catch fish for themselves and might also keep a lookout for ships.

But things went from bad to worse. The Native people there grew daily bolder, and the colonists lived constantly in dread of an attack from them.

At length, although he had tried hard to avoid it, Lane determined to fight them. They were easily overcome and fled to the woods. But Lane knew well that his advantage was only for the moment. Should help not come, the colony would be wiped out. Then one day, about a week after the fight, news was brought to Lane that a great fleet of twenty-three ships had appeared in the distance.

Were they friends, or were they foes? That was the great question. The English knew the terrible story of Fort Caroline. Were these Spanish ships? Fearing that they might be, Ralph Lane looked to his defenses, and made ready to withstand the enemy, if enemy they proved to be, as bravely as might be.

But soon it was seen that their fears were needless, the ships were English, and two days later, Sir Francis Drake anchored in the wretched little harbor.

Drake had not come on purpose to relieve the colony. He had been out on one of his marauding expeditions against the Spaniards. He had taken and sacked St. Domingo, Cartagena, and Fort St. Augustine. And now, sailing home in triumph, chance had brought him to Raleigh's colony at Roanoke. And when he saw the miserable condition of the colonists, and heard the tale of their hardships, he offered to take them all home to England. Or, he said, if they chose to remain, he would leave them a ship and food and everything that was necessary to keep them from want until help should come.

Both Lane and his chief officers who were men of spirit wanted to stay. So they accepted Drake's offer of the loan of a ship, agreeing that after they had found a good place for a colony and a better harbor, they would go home to England and return again the next year.

Thus the matter was settled. Drake began to put provisions on board one of his ships for the use of the colony. The colonists on their side began writing letters to send home with Drake's ships. All was business and excitement. But in the midst of it, a great storm arose. It lasted for four days and was so violent that most of Drake's ships were forced to put out to sea, lest they should be dashed to pieces upon the shore.

Among the ships thus driven out to sea was that which Drake had promised to give Ralph Lane. And when the storm was over, it was nowhere to be seen.

So Drake offered another ship to Lane. It was a large one, too large to get into the little harbor, but the only one he could spare. Lane was now doubtful what was best to do. Did it not seem as if by driving away their ship God had stretched out His hand to take them from thence? Was the storm not meant as a sign to them?

So not being able to decide by himself what was best to do, Lane called his officers and gentlemen together, and asked advice of them.

They all begged him to go home. No help had come from Sir Richard Grenville, nor was it likely to come, for Drake had brought the news that war between Spain and England had been declared. They knew that at such a time every Englishman would bend all his energies to the defeat of Spain, and that Raleigh would have neither thoughts nor money to spare for that far-off colony.

At length it was settled that they should all go home. In haste then, the Englishmen got on board, for Drake was anxious to be gone from the dangerous anchorage which "sustained more peril of wreck," says Ralph Lane, "than all his former most honorable actions against the Spaniards, with praises unto God for all."

So on the 19th of June, 1586, the colonists set sail and arrived in England some six weeks later. They brought with them two things which afterward proved to be of great importance. The first was tobacco. The use of it had been known ever since the days of Columbus, but it was now for the first time brought to England. The second was the potato. This Raleigh planted on his estates in Ireland, and to this day Ireland still produces potatoes.

But meanwhile Raleigh had not forgotten his colonists, and scarce a week after they had sailed away, a ship arrived "freighted with all manner of things in the most plentiful manner for the supply and relief of his colony."

For some time, the ship beat up and down the coast, searching vainly for the colony. And at length finding no sign of it, it returned to England. About a fortnight later, Sir Richard Grenville also arrived with three ships. To his astonishment when he reached Roanoke, he saw no sign of the ship which he knew had sailed shortly before him. And to his still greater astonishment, he found the colony deserted. Yet he could not believe that it had been abandoned. So he searched the country up and down in the hope of finding some of the colonists. But finding no trace of them, he at length gave up the search and returned to the forsaken huts. And being unwilling to lose possession of the country, he determined to leave some of his men there. So fifteen men were left behind, well provided with everything necessary to keep them for two years. Then Sir Richard sailed homeward.

In spite of all these mischances, Raleigh would not give up his great idea. And the following year, he fitted out another expedition. This time there were a few women among the colonists, and John White, who had already been out with Lane, was chosen as Governor.

It was now decided to give up Roanoke, which had proved such an unfortunate spot, and the new company of colonists was bound for Chesapeake Bay. But before they settled there, they were told to go to Roanoke to pick up the fifteen men left by Sir Richard Grenville and take them to Chesapeake also.

When, however, they reached Roanoke, the Master of the vessels, who was by birth a Spaniard, and who was perhaps in league with the Spanish, said that it was too late in the year to go seeking another spot. So whether they would or not, he landed the colonists and sailed away, leaving only one small boat with them.

Thus perforce they had to take up their abode in the old spot. They found it deserted. The fort was razed to the ground, and although the huts were still standing, they were choked with weeds and over-grown with wild vines, while deer wandered in and out of the open doors. It was plain that for many months no man had lived there. And although careful search was made, saving the bones of one, no sign was found of the fifteen men left there by Sir Richard. At length the new colonists learned from the Indians that they had been traitor-ously set upon by hostile tribes. Most of them were slain; the others escaped in their boat and went no man knew whither.

The Englishmen were very angry when they heard that and wanted to punish the Native people. So they set out against them. But the people had fled at their coming, and the Englishmen instead killed some of the friendly inhabitants, instead of their enemies. Thus things were made worse instead of better.

And now amid all these troubles, on the 18th of August 1587, a little girl was born. Her father was Ananias Dare, and her mother was the daughter of John White, the Governor. The little baby was thus the granddaughter of the Governor, and because she was the first English child to be born in Virginia, she was called Virginia.

But matters were not going well in the colony. Day by day the men were finding out things which were lacking, and which they felt they must have if they were not all to perish. So a few days after Virginia was christened, all the chief men came to the Governor and begged him to go back to England to get fresh supplies and other things necessary to the life of the colony. John White, however, refused to go. The next day not only the men but the women also came to him and again begged him to go back to England. They begged so hard that at last the Governor consented to go.

All were agreed that the place they were now in was by no means the best which might be chosen for a colony, and it had been determined that they should move some fifty miles further inland. Now it was arranged that if they moved while Governor White was away, they should carve on the trees and posts of the door the name of the place to which they had gone, so that on his return he might be able easily to find them. And also it was arranged that if they were in any trouble or distress, they should carve a cross over the name.

All these matters being settled, John White set forth. And it was with great content that the colonists saw their Governor go. For they knew that they could send home no better man to look after their welfare, and they were sure he would bring back the food and other things which were needed.

But when White arrived in England, he found that no man, not even Raleigh, had a thought to spare for Virginia. For Spain was making ready all her mighty sea power to crush England. And the English were straining every nerve to meet and break that power. So John White had to wait with what patience he could. Often his heart was sick when he thought of his daughter and his little granddaughter, Virginia Dare, far away in that great unknown land across the sea. Often he longed to be back beside them. But his longings were of no avail. He could but wait. For every ship was seized by Government and pressed into the service of the country. And while the Spaniards were at the gate, it was accounted treason for any Englishman to sail to western lands.

So the summer of 1588 passed, the autumn came, and at length the great Armada sailed from Spain. It sailed across the narrow seas in pride and splendor, haughtily certain of crushing the insolent sea dogs of England. But as the weather changed, "God blew with His breath and they were scattered." Before many days were over, these proud ships were fleeing before the storm, their sails torn, their masts splintered. They were shattered upon the rocky shores of Scotland and Ireland. They were swallowed by the deep.

The sea power of Spain was broken, and the history of America truly began. For as has been said, "The defeat of the Invincible Armada was the opening event in the history of the United States."

Free now from the dread of Spain, ships could come and go without hindrance. But another year and more passed before John White succeeded in getting ships and provisions and setting out once more for Virginia.

It was for him an anxious voyage, but as he neared the place where the colony had been, his heart rejoiced, for he saw smoke rising from the land. It was dark, however, before they reached the spot, and seeing no lights save that of a huge fire far in the woods, the Governor sounded a trumpet call. The notes of the trumpet rang through the woods and died away to silence. Answer there was none. So the men called and called again, but still no answer came. Then with sinking heart, John White bade them sing some well-known English songs. For that, he thought, would surely bring an answer from the shore.

So through the still night air the musical sound of men's voices rang out. But still no answer came from the silent fort. With a heart heavy as lead, the Governor waited for the dawn. As soon as it was light, he went ashore. The fort was deserted. Grass and weeds grew in the ruined houses. But upon a post "in fair capital letters" was carved the word "Croatoan." This was the name of a neighboring island inhabited by a tribe friendly to the Englishmen. There was no cross or sign of distress carved over the letters. And when Governor White saw that, he was greatly comforted.

He spent some time searching about for other signs of the colonists. In one place he found some iron and lead thrown aside as if too heavy to carry away, and now overgrown with weeds. In another, he found five chests which had evidently been buried by the colonists but had been dug up again by the Indians.

They had been burst open and the contents lay scattered about the grass. Three of these chests John White saw were his own, and it grieved him greatly to see his things spoiled and broken. His books were torn from their covers, his watercolor pictures and maps were rotten with the rain, and his armor almost eaten through with rust.

At length, having searched in vain for any other signs of the colonists, the English returned to the ships and set sail for Croatoan.

But now they encountered terrible storms. Their ships were battered this way and that, their sails were torn, their anchors lost. And at length in spite of all entreaties, the captain resolved to make sail for England. So John White never saw Croatoan, never knew what had become of his dear ones. And what happened to little Virginia Dare, the first English girl to be born on the soil of what would become the United States, will never be known. But years afterwards, settlers were told by the Native people that the Englishmen left at Roanoke had gone to live among the various tribes. For some years, it was said, they lived in a friendly manner together but that in time, however, the Native people began to hate the Englishmen and caused them all to be slain, except four men, one young woman, and three boys. Was the young woman perhaps Virginia Dare? No one can tell.

All Raleigh's attempts at founding a colony had thus come to nothing. Still he did not despair. Once again he sent out an expedition. But that, too, failed and the leader returned, having done nothing. Even this did not break Raleigh's faith in the future of Virginia. "I shall yet live to see it an English Nation," he wrote.

But although Raleigh's faith was as firm as before, his money was gone. He had spent enormous sums on his fruitless efforts to found a colony. Now he had no more to spend.

And now great changes came. Good Queen Bess died, and James of Scotland reigned in her stead. Raleigh fell into disgrace, was imprisoned in the Tower, and after a short release was beheaded there. Thus an end came to all his splendid schemes. Never before, perhaps, had such noble devotion to King and country been so basely requited. One of the judges at his trial later said that "the justice of England has never been so degraded and injured as by the condemnation of the honourable Sir Walter Raleigh." No man is perfect, nor was Raleigh perfect. But he was a great man, and although all his plans failed, we remember him as the first Englishman to gain possession of any part of North America.

Notes:

Captain Barlowe's description of the land and its people is taken from Richard Hakluyt, The Principal Voyages, Traffiques, and Discourses of the English Nations, *1599-1600.*

In History of North Carolina: Embracing the period between the first voyage to the colony in 1584, to the last in 1591, *by Francis L. Hawks, 1857, there is a reprint from Hakluyt, believed to be written by M. Arthur Barlowe, which says,*

As to this name, Wingandacoa, it never was the Indian name of the country, but was misapplied to it by a mistake of the English. Sir Walter himself, in his History of the World, tells us so. In speaking of Peru, Yucatan, and Paria, after showing that these names were but words of the native language, which the Spaniards mistook for names of the place, he thus proceeds: "The same happened among the English, which I sent under Sir Richard Grenville to inhabit Virginia. For when some of my people asked the name of the country, one of the savages" [who, of course, did not understand the query of the English] "answered 'Win-gan-da-coa,' which is as much as to say, 'You wear good clothes,' or 'gay clothes.'"

Some historians believe the missing silver cup was likely a communion chalice.

Ralph Lane's quote about Drake is taken from The Colony At Roanoke *by Ralph Lane, 1586.*

The quote about Raleigh's third sponsored voyage is from History of North Carolina: Embracing the period between the first voyage to the colony in 1584, to the last in 1591, *by Francis L. Hawks, 1857.*

"God blew with His breath and they were scattered," is from the Latin inscribed on the commemorative medal celebrating the defeat of the Armada, "Flavit Jehovah et Dissipati Sunt."

Raleigh's quote about the future of Virginia is from a letter about America to Sir Robert Cecil.

Pronunciation Guide:

Croatoan – crow-uh-TOE-un

Wanchese- wahn-CHEES

Algonquian – al-GONG-kwee-in

Aquascogoc – ah-KWAH-skuh-goc

Chapter 13

The Adventures of Captain John Smith

Raleigh was the true father of England beyond the seas. He was a great statesman and patriot. But he was a dreamer, too, and all his schemes failed. Other men followed him who likewise failed. But it would take too long to tell of them all, of Bartholomew Gosnold who led the first expedition to Martha's Vineyard and Cape Cod and named them both; of Bartholomew Gilbert, brave Sir Humphrey's son, who was slain in a conflict with Algonquians while searching for the lost Roanoke colonists, and of many more besides.

Again and again men tried to plant a colony on the shores of America. Again and again they failed. But with British doggedness they went on trying, and at length succeeded.

Raleigh lay in the Tower of London, a prisoner accused of treason. All his lands were taken from him. Virginia, which had been granted to him by Queen Elizabeth, was the King's once more to give to whom he would. So now two companies were formed, one of London merchants called the London Company, one of Plymouth merchants called the Plymouth Company. And both these companies prayed King James to grant them permission to found colonies in Virginia. Virginia, therefore, was divided into two parts; the right to found colonies in the southern half being given to the London Company, the right to found colonies in the northern half being given to the Plymouth Company, upon condition that the colonies founded must be one hundred miles distant from each other.

These companies were formed by merchants. They were formed for trade and in the hope of making money, in spite of the fact that up to this time no man had made money by trying to found colonies in America, but on the contrary many had lost fortunes.

Of the two companies now formed, it was only the London Company which really did anything. The Plymouth Company indeed sent out an expedition which reached Virginia. But the Popham Colony was a failure, and after a year of hardships the colonists set sail for England, taking home with them such doleful accounts of their sufferings that none who heard them ever wished to help to found a colony.

The expedition of the London Company had a better fate. It was in December, 1606, that the little fleet of three ships, the *Susan Constant*, the *Godspeed* and the *Discovery,* put out from England, and turned westward towards the New World.

With the expedition sailed Captain John Smith. He was bronzed and bearded, a swaggering, longheaded, lovable sort of man, ambitious, too, and not given to submit his will to others. Since a boy of sixteen he had led a wandering adventurous life - a life crammed full of heroic deeds, of hairbreadth escapes of which we have no space to tell here. But I hope someday you will read his own story of these days. For he was a writer as well as a warrior, and "what his sword did his pen wrote." Every American boy and girl should read his story, for he has been called the first American writer.

Now with this saucy, swaggering fellow on board, troubles were not far to seek. The voyage was long and tedious. For six weeks, adverse winds kept the little fleet prisoner in the English Channel within sight of English shores, a thing trying to the tempers of men used to action and burning with impatience to reach the land beyond the seas. They lay idle with nothing to do but talk. So they fell to discussing matters about the colony they were to found. And from discussing they fell to disputing, until it ended at length in a bitter quarrel between Smith and another of the adventurers, Captain Edward Wingfield.

Captain Wingfield was twice John Smith's age and deemed that he knew much better how a colony ought to be formed than this dictatorial youth of twenty-seven. He himself was just as dictatorial and narrow into the bargain. So between the two the voyage was by no means peaceful.

Good Master Hunt, the preacher who went with the expedition in spite of the fact that he was so weak and ill that few thought he would live, did his best to still the angry passions.

To some extent he succeeded. And when a fair wind blew at length the ships spread their sails to it and were soon out of sight of England. Two months of storm and danger passed before the adventurers sighted the West Indies. Here they went ashore on the island of San Dominica. Delighted once more to see land and escape from the confinement of the ship, they stayed three weeks among the sunny islands. They hunted and fished, traded with the Native people, boiled pork in hot natural springs, feasted on fresh food and vegetables, and generally enjoyed themselves.

But among all this merry-making, Wingfield did not forget his anger against John Smith. Their quarrels became so bad that Wingfield decided to end both the quarrels and John Smith. So he ordered a gallows to be set up and, having accused Smith of mutiny, made ready to hang him. But John Smith stoutly defended himself. Nothing could be proved against him. He laughed at the gallows, and as he quaintly put it, "could not be persuaded to use them."

Nevertheless, although nothing could be proved against him, there were many who quite agreed that Captain John Smith was a turbulent fellow. So to keep him quiet they clapped him in irons and kept him so until their arrival in Virginia. After leaving the West Indies, the adventurers fell into more bad weather, and lost their course, but finally they arrived safely in Chesapeake Bay.

They named the capes on either side Henry and Charles, in honor of the two sons of their King. Upon Cape Henry, they set up a brass cross upon which was carved "Jacobus Rex" for King James, and thus they claimed the land for England. Then they sailed on up the river which they named James River, in honor of the King himself. Their settlement they named Jamestown, also in his honor. Jamestown has now disappeared, but the two capes and the river are still called by the names given them by these early settlers.

Before this expedition sailed, the directors of the Company had arranged who among the colonists were to be the rulers. But for some quaint reason, they were not told. Their names, together with many instructions as to what they were to do, were put into a sealed box, and orders were given that this box was not to be opened until Virginia was reached.

The box was now opened, and it was found that John Smith was named among the seven who were to form the council. The others were much disgusted at this, and in spite of all he could say, they refused to have him in the council. They did, however, set him free from his fetters. Of the council, Wingfield was chosen President. All the others, except John Smith, took oath to do their best for the colony. Then at once the business of building houses was begun. While the council drew plans, the men dug trenches and felled trees in order to clear space on which to pitch their tents, or otherwise busied themselves about the settlement.

The Powhatan people appeared to the Englishmen to be friendly, and they often came to look on curiously at their strange doings. And Wingfield thought them so gentle and kindly that he would not allow the men to build any fortifications except a sort of screen of interwoven boughs.

Besides building houses, one of the colonists' first cares was to provide themselves with a church. But indeed it was one of the quaintest churches ever known. An old sail was stretched beneath a group of trees to give shelter from the burning sun. And to make a pulpit, a plank of wood was nailed between two trees which grew near together. And here good Master Hunt preached twice every Sunday while the men sat on felled trunks, reverently listening to his long sermons.

While the houses were being built, Smith, with some twenty others, was sent to explore the country. They sailed up the river and found the Indians to all appearance friendly. But they found no gold or precious stones and could hear nothing of a passage to the Pacific Ocean which they had been told to seek. So they returned to Jamestown. Arriving here they found that the day before, some of the Powhatans had attacked the settlement and that one English boy lay slain and seventeen men were injured.

This was a bitter disappointment to Wingfield who had trusted in the friendliness of the Powhatan. But at length he was persuaded to allow fortifications to be built. Even then, however, the colonists were not secure, for as they went about their business felling trees or digging the ground, the Native men would shoot at them from the shelter of the surrounding forest. If a man strayed from the fort, he was sure to return wounded, if he returned at all; and in this sort of warfare the stolid English were no match for the swift Indians. "Our men," says Smith, "by their disorderly straggling were often hurt, when the savages by the nimbleness of their heels well escaped."

So six months passed, and the ships which had brought out the colonists were ready to go back to England with a cargo of wood instead of the gold which the Company had hoped for. But before the ships sailed, Smith, who was still considered in disgrace, and therefore kept out of the council, insisted on having a fair trial. For he would not have Captain Newport go home and spread evil stories about him.

Smith's enemies were unwilling to allow the trial. But Smith would take no denial. So at length his request was granted, the result being that he was proved innocent of every charge against him and was at length admitted to the council.

Now at last something like peace was restored, and Captain Newport set sail for home. He promised to make all speed he could and to be back in five months' time. And indeed he had need to hasten. For the journey outward had been so long, the supply of food so scant, that already it was giving out. And when Captain Newport sailed, it was plain that the colonists had not food enough to last fifteen weeks.

Such food it was, too! It consisted chiefly of worm-eaten grain. A pint was served out daily for each man, and this boiled and made into a sort of porridge formed their chief food. Their drink was cold water. For tea and coffee were unknown in those days, and beer they had none. To men used to the beer and beef of England in plenty, this indeed seemed meager diet. "Had we been as free of all sins as gluttony and drunkenness," says Smith, "we might have been canonized for saints." He said that their wheat had "fried some twenty-six weeks in the ship's hold, contained as many worms as grains, so that we might truly call it rather so much bran than corn; our drink was water, our lodgings castles in the air."

There was fish enough in the river, game enough in the woods. But the birds and beasts were so wild, and the men so unskillful and ignorant in ways of shooting and trapping, that they succeeded in catching very little. Besides which there were few among the colonists who had any idea of what work meant. More than half the company were "gentlemen adventurers," daredevil, shiftless men who had joined the expedition in search of excitement with no idea of laboring with their hands.

Badly fed, unused to the heat of a Virginian summer, the men soon fell ill. Their tents were rotten, their houses yet unbuilt. Trees remained unfelled, the land untilled, while the men lay on the bare ground about the fort, groaning and in misery. Many died, and soon those who remained were so feeble that they had scarce strength to bury the dead or even to crawl to the "common kettle" for their daily measure of porridge.

In their misery the men became suspicious and jealous, and once more quarrels were rife. Wingfield had never been loved. Now many grew to hate him, for they believed that while they starved, he kept back for his own use secret stores of oil and wine and other dainties. No explanations were of any avail, and he was deposed from his office of President and another chosen in his place.

As autumn drew on, the misery began to lessen. For the Powhatan, whose corn was now ripe, began to bring it to the fort to barter it for chisels, and beads, and other trifles. Wild fowl, too, such as ducks and geese, swarmed in the river.

So with good food and cooler weather, the sick soon began to mend. Energy returned to them, and once more they found strength to build and thatch their houses. And led by Smith, they made many expeditions among the different Powhatan tribes, bringing back great stores of venison, wild turkeys, bread, and grain in exchange for beads, hatchets, bells and other knick-knacks.

But all the misery through which the colonists had passed had taught them nothing. They took no thought for the time to come when food might again be scarce. They took no care of it, but feasted daily on good bread, fish and fowl and "wild beasts as fat as we could eat them," says Smith.

Now one December day, Smith set out on an exploring expedition up the Chickahominy River. It was a hard journey, for the river was so overgrown with trees that the men had to hew a path for the little vessel. At length the bark could go no further, so Smith left it, and went on in a canoe with only two Englishmen and two Native men as guides.

For a time, all went well. But one day he and his companions went ashore to camp. While the others were preparing a meal, Smith, taking one of the Native men with him, went on to explore a little further. But he had not gone far when he heard a wild, blood-curdling war whoop. Guessing at once that warriors had come against him, he resolved to sell his life as dearly as might be. So seizing the Native guide he tied his arm fast to his own with his garters. Then with pistol in his right hand and holding the man in front of him as a shield, he pushed as rapidly as he could in the direction of the camp.

Arrows flew round him thick and fast, but Smith's good buff coat turned them aside. The whole forest was alive with archers, but although from the shelter of the trees they showered arrows upon Smith, none dared approach him to take him. For they knew and dreaded the terrible fire stick which he held in his hand. Smith fired again and yet again as he retreated, and more than one attacker fell, never more to rise. He kept his eyes upon the bushes and trees trying to catch glimpses of the enemies as they skulked among them, and he paid little heed to the path he was taking. So suddenly he found himself floundering in a quagmire.

Still he fought for dear life, and as long as he held his pistol none dared come near to take him. But at length, chilled and wet, and half dead-with cold, unable to go further, he saw it was useless to resist longer. So he tossed away his pistol. At once the Powhatans closed in upon him and, dragging him out of the quagmire, led him to their chief.

Smith had given in because he knew that one man stuck in a quagmire could not hope to keep three hundred warriors long at bay. But he had sharp wits as well as a steady hand, and with them he still fought for his life. As soon as he was brought before the chief, he whipped out his compass, and showing it to the chief, explained to him that it always pointed north, and thus the Englishmen were able to find their way through the pathless desert.

To the Powhatans this seemed like magic; they marveled greatly at the shining needle which they could see so plainly and yet not touch. Seeing their interest, Smith went on to explain other marvels of the sun, and moon, and stars, and the roundness of the earth, until those who heard were quite sure he was a great "medicine man."

Thus Smith fought for his life. But at length utterly exhausted, he could say no more. So while the chief still held the little ivory compass, and watched the quivering needle, his followers led Smith away to his own campfire. Here lay the other Englishmen dead, thrust through with many arrows. And here the Powhatans warmed and chafed his benumbed body and treated him with all the kindness they knew. But that brought Smith little comfort. For he knew it was their way. A famous warrior might be sure of kindness at their hands if they meant in the end to slay him with awful torture.

And so, thoroughly warmed and restored, in less than an hour Smith found himself fast bound to a tree, while grim warriors, terribly painted, danced around him, bows and arrows in hand. They were about to slay him when the chief, holding up the compass, bade them lay down their weapons. Such a "medicine man," he had decided, must not thus be slain. So Smith was unbound.

For some weeks Smith was marched hither and thither from village to village. He was kindly enough treated, but he never knew how long the kindness would last, and he constantly expected death. Yet he was quite calm. He kept a journal, and in this he set down accounts of many strange sights he saw, not knowing if indeed they would ever be read.

At length Smith was brought to the birchbark house of the great Powhatan, the chief of chiefs, or Emperor, as these simple English folk called him. To receive his prisoner, the Powhatan put on his greatest bravery. Feathered and painted and wearing a wide robe of raccoon skins, he sat upon a broad couch beside a fire. On either side of him sat one of his wives and behind in grim array stood his warriors, row upon row. Behind them again stood the women. Their faces and shoulders were painted bright red, about their necks they wore chains of white beads, and on their heads the down of white birds.

It was a weird scene, and the flickering firelight added to its strangeness. Silent and still as statues, the warriors stood. Then as John Smith was led before the emperor, they raised a wild shout. As that died away to silence, one of the Powhatan's women rose and brought a basin of water to Smith. In this he washed his hands, and then another woman brought him a bunch of feathers instead of a towel, with which to dry them.

After this the Powhatans feasted their prisoner with all their abundance. Then a long consultation took place. What was said, Smith knew not. He only knew that his life hung in the balance. The end of the consultation he felt sure meant life or death for him.

At length the long talk came to an end. Two great stones were placed before the emperor. Then as many as could lay hands on Smith seized him, and dragging him to the stones, they threw him on the ground, and laid his head upon them. Fiercely then they brandished their clubs and Smith knew that his last hour had come, and that the Powhatans were about to beat out his brains.

But the raised clubs never fell, for with a cry Pocahontas, the emperor's young daughter, sprang through the circle of warriors. She stood beside the prisoner, pleading for his life. But the Powhatans were in no mood to listen to prayers for mercy. So seeing that all her entreaties were in vain, she threw herself upon her knees beside Smith, put her arms about his neck, and laid her head upon his, crying out that if they would beat out his brains, they should beat hers out, too.

Of all his many children, the Powhatan loved this little daughter best. He could deny her nothing. So Smith's life was saved. He should live, said the Powhatan, to make hatchets for him, and bells and beads for his little daughter.

Having thus been saved, Smith was looked upon as one of the tribe. Two days later he was admitted as such with fearsome ceremony.

Having painted and decorated himself as frightfully as he could, the Powhatan caused Smith to be taken to a large dwelling in the forest. The house was divided in two by a curtain, and in one half a huge fire burned. Smith was placed upon a mat in front of the fire and left alone. He did not understand in the least what was going on and marveled greatly what this new ceremony might mean. But he had not sat long before the fire when he heard doleful sounds coming from the other side of the curtain. Then from behind it appeared the Powhatan with a hundred others as hideously painted as himself, and told Smith that now that they were brothers, he might go back to his fort.

So with twelve guides Smith set out. Yet in spite of all their feasting and ceremonies, Smith scarcely believed in the friendship of the Native people, and no one was more surprised than himself when he at length reached Jamestown in safety.

Notes:

"Virginia" was the term used to describe the east coast of what is now Florida, all the way to Canada.

Popham Colony, also called Sagadahoc Colony, was in modern-day Maine. Remarkably, only one colonist died, but it was their leader and the ship's captain, George Popham. Popham Colony was named for its financial backer, Sir John Popham, a relative of George Popham.

Captain John Smith's quotes can be found in his volumes **The Generall Historie of Virginia, New England & the Summer Isles: Together with The True Travels, Adventures and Observations, and a Sea Grammar** *(London, 1624).*

Note from Project Gutenberg: The emperor's name was Wahunsunakok, the name of the tribe Powhatan, and the English called the emperor the Powhatan.

While the story of Pocahontas saving John Smith has been debated for years, it remains a part of the story of America's founding. Whether it happened exactly as retold, or whether John Smith misinterpreted that event, the fact that Pocahontas saved his life a later time (told in chapter 14) has never been challenged.

The Powhatan lived in a house called a yehakin.

Pronunciation Guide:

Powhatan – POW-huh-tan

Chapter 14

More Adventures of Captain John Smith

Smith had been away from the settlement nearly a month, and he returned to find the colony in confusion and misery. Many had died, and those who remained were quarreling among themselves. Indeed some were on the point of deserting and sneaking off to England in the one little ship they had. They were not in the least pleased to see Smith return, and they resolved once more to get rid of him. So they accused him of causing the death of the two men who had gone with him, and condemned him to death. Thus Smith had only escaped from the hands of the Powhatans to be murdered by his own people.

The order went forth. He was to be hanged next day.

But suddenly all was changed, for a man looking out to sea saw a white sail. "Ship ahoy!" he shouted. "Ship ahoy!"

At the joyful sound the men forgot their bickerings, and hurrying to the shore, welcomed the new arrival. It was Captain Newport with his long-promised help. He soon put a stop to the hanging business, and he also set poor Captain Wingfield free. For he had been kept prisoner ever since he had been deposed.

Newport had brought food for the colony, but he had also brought many new settlers. Unfortunately, too, one day the storehouse was set on fire, and much of the grain was destroyed. So that in spite of the new supplies the colony would soon again have been in the old starving condition, had it not been for Pocahontas. She was resolved that her beloved Captain Smith should want for nothing, and now every four or five days she came to the fort laden with provisions.

Smith also took Captain Newport to visit the Powhatan people, and great barter was made of blue beads and tinsel ornaments for grain and foodstuffs.

After a time, Captain Newport sailed home again, taking the deposed President Wingfield with him. He took home also great tales of the Emperor Powhatan's might and splendor. And King James was so impressed with what he heard that he made up his mind that Powhatan should be crowned. So in autumn Captain Newport returned again to Jamestown, bringing with him more settlers, among them two women. He also brought a crown and other presents to Powhatan from King James, together with a command for his coronation. So Smith made a journey to Powhatan's village of Werowocomoco and begged him to come to Jamestown to receive his presents. But Powhatan refused to go, for he was suspicious and stood upon his dignity.

"If your King has sent me presents," he said, "I also am a king, and this is my land. Eight days will I wait here to receive them. Your Father Newport must come to me, not I to him."

So with this answer Smith went back and seeing nothing else for it, Captain Newport set out for Powhatan's village with the presents. He did not in the least want to go, but the King had commanded that Powhatan was to be crowned. And the King had to be obeyed. He arrived safely at Werowocomoco, and the next day was appointed for the coronation.

First the presents were brought out and set in order. There was a great four-poster bed with hangings and curtains of damask, a basin and ewer and other costly novelties such as never before had been seen in these lands.

After the gifts had been presented, the Englishmen tried to place a fine red cloak on Powhatan's shoulders. But he would not have it. He resisted all their attempts until at last one of the other chiefs persuaded him that it would not hurt him, so at last he submitted.

Next the crown was produced. Powhatan had never seen a crown, and had no idea of its use, nor could he be made to understand that he must kneel to have it put on.

"A foul trouble there was," says one of the settlers who writes about it. No persuasions or explanations were of any avail. The Englishmen knelt down in front of him to show him what he must do. They explained, they persuaded, until they were worn out. It was all in vain. The Powhatan remained as stolid as a mule. Kneel he would not.

So at length, seeing nothing else for it, three of them took the crown in their hands, and the others pressed with all their weight upon the Powhatan's shoulders so that they forced him to stoop a little, and thus, amid howls of laughter, the crown was hastily thrust on his head. As soon as it was done the soldiers fired a volley in honor of the occasion. At the sound the newly-crowned monarch started up in terror, casting aside the men who held him. But when he saw that no one was killed, and that those around him were laughing, he soon recovered from his fright. And thanking them gravely for their presents, he pompously handed his old shoes and his raccoon cloak to Captain Newport as a present for King James. Thus this strangest of all coronations came to an end.

This senseless ceremony did no good, but rather harm. The Emperor Powhatan had resisted being crowned with all his might, but afterwards he was much puffed up about it, and began to think much more of himself, and much less of the Englishmen.

Among others, Smith thought it was nothing but a piece of tom-foolery and likely to bring trouble ere long.

For some months now he had been President, and as President he wrote to the London Company, "For the coronation of Powhatan," he said, "by whose advice you sent him such presents I know not, but this give me leave to tell you: I fear they will be the confusion of us all, ere we hear from you again."

Smith told the Company other plain truths. They had been sending out all sorts of idle fine gentlemen who had never done a day's work in their lives. They could not fell a tree, and when they tried, the axe blistered their tender fingers. Some of them worked indeed cheer-fully enough, but it took ten of them to do as much work as one good workman. Others were simply stirrers up of mischief. One of these Smith now sent back to England "lest the company should cut his throat." And Smith begged the Company to keep those sort of people at home in the future, and send him carpenters and gardeners, black-smiths and masons, and people who could do something.

Captain Newport now sailed home, and Smith was left to govern the colony and find food for the many hungry mouths. He went as usual to trade with the Powhatans. But he found them no longer willing to barter their corn for a little copper or a handful of beads. They now wanted swords and guns. The Powhatan Emperor, too, grew weary of seeing the newcomers on the land of which he was crowned king. He forgot his vows of friendship with Smith. All he wanted was to see the Englishmen leave his country. And the best way to get rid of them was to starve them.

But although Powhatan had grown tired of seeing the Englishmen stride like lords through his land, he yet greatly admired them. And now he wanted more than anything else to have a house, a palace as it seemed to him, with windows and fireplaces like those they built for themselves at Jamestown. For in the little Native houses which his followers could build, there was no room for the splendid furniture which had been sent to him for his coronation. So now he sent to Smith asking him to send men to build a house. Smith at once sent some men to begin the work, and soon followed with others.

On their way to the Powhatan's town, Smith and his companions stopped a night with another friendly chief who warned them to beware of Powhatan.

"You will find him use you well," he said. "But trust him not. And be sure he hath no chance to seize your arms. For he hath sent for you only to cut your throats."

However in spite of this warning, Smith decided to go on. So he thanked the friendly chief for his good counsel, and assuring him that he would love him always for it, he went on his way.

It was wintertime now, and the rivers were half frozen over, the land was covered with snow, and icy winds blew over it. Indeed the weather was so bad that for a week Smith and his men could not go on, but had to take refuge with some friendly Indians. Here in the warm bark-huts they were cozy and jolly. The Indians treated them kindly, and fed them well on oysters, fish, game and wildfowl. Christmas came and went while they were with these kindly people, and at length, the weather becoming a little better, they decided to push on. After many adventures, they reached Powhatan's village. They were very weary from their long cold journey and taking possession of the first houses they came to, they sent a message to Powhatan, telling him that they had come, and asking him to send food.

This the old emperor immediately did, and soon they were dining royally on bread, venison and turkeys. The next day, too, Powhatan sent them supplies of food. Then he calmly asked how long they were going to stay, and when they would be gone.

At this Smith was greatly astonished, for had not Powhatan sent for him?

"I did not send for you," said the wily old man, "and if you have come for corn I have none to give you, still less have my people. But," he added slyly, "if perchance you have forty swords, I might find forty baskets of corn in exchange for them."

"You did not send for me?" said Smith in astonishment. "How can that be? For I have with me the messengers you sent to ask me to come, and they can vouch for the truth of it. I marvel that you can be so forgetful."

Then, seeing that he could not fool the Englishmen, the old chief laughed merrily, pretending that he had only been joking. But still he held to it that he would give no corn except in exchange for guns and swords.

"Powhatan," answered Smith, "believing your promises to satisfy my wants, and out of love to you I sent you my men for your building, thereby neglecting mine own needs. Now by these strange demands you think to undo us and bring us to want indeed. For you know well as I have told you long ago, of guns and swords I have none to spare. Yet steal from you or wrong you I will not, nor yet break that friendship which we have promised each other, unless by bad usage you force me thereto."

When Powhatan heard Smith speak thus firmly, he pretended to give way and promised that within two days the English should have all the corn he and his people could spare. But he added, "My people fear to bring you corn seeing you are all armed, for they say you come not hither for trade, but to invade my country and take possession of it. Therefore, to free us of this fear lay aside your weapons, for indeed here they are needless, we being all friends."

With such and many more cunning words Powhatan sought to make Captain Smith and his men lay aside their arms. But to all his persuasions Smith turned a deaf ear.

"Nay," he said, "we have no thought of revenge or cruelty against you. When your people come to us at Jamestown we receive them with their bows and arrows. With you it must be the same. We wear our arms even as our clothes."

So seeing that he could not gain his end, the old chief gave in. Yet one more effort he made to soften the Englishman's heart.

"I have never honored any chief as I have you," he said, with a sigh, "yet you show me less kindness than anyone. You call me father, but you do just as you like."

Smith, however, would waste no more time parleying, and gave orders for his men to fetch the corn. But while he was busy with this, Powhatan slipped away and gathered his warriors. Then suddenly in the midst of their business, Smith and one or two others found themselves cut off from their comrades and surrounded by a yelling crowd of painted warriors. Instantly the Englishmen drew their swords and, charging into the enemy, put them to flight. Seeing how easily their warriors had been routed and how strong the Englishmen were, the chiefs tried to make friends with them again, pretending that the attack upon them was a mistake, and that no evil against them had been intended.

The Englishmen, however, put no more trust in their words and sternly, with loaded guns and drawn swords in hand, bade them to talk no more, but make haste and load their boat with corn. And so thoroughly cowed were the Powhatans by the fierce words and looks of the Englishmen that they needed no second bidding. Hastily laying down their bows and arrows they bent their backs to the work, their one desire now being to get rid as soon as possible of these fierce and powerful intruders.

When the work was done, however, it was too late to sail that night, for the tide was low. So the Englishmen returned to the house in which they lodged, to rest till morning and wait for high water.

Meanwhile Powhatan had by no means given up his desire for revenge, and while the Englishmen sat by their fire, he plotted to slay them all. But as he talked with his men, Pocahontas listened. And when she heard that the great English Chief whom she loved so dearly was to be killed, her heart was filled with grief, and she resolved to save him. So silently she slipped out into the dark night and, trembling lest she should be discovered, was soon speeding through the wild lonesome forest towards the Englishmen's hut. Reaching it in safety she burst in upon them as they sat in the firelight waiting for the Powhatan to send their supper.

"You must not wait," she cried, "you must go at once. My father is gathering all his force against you. He will indeed send you a great feast, but those who bring it have orders to slay you, and any who escape them he is ready with his braves to slay. Oh, if you would live you must flee at once," and as she spoke the tears ran down her cheeks.

The Englishmen were truly grateful to Pocahontas for her warning. They thanked her warmly and would have laden her with gifts of beads and colored cloth, and such things as the Powhatans delighted in, but she would not take them.

"I dare not take such things," she said. "For if my father saw me with them he would know that I had come here to warn you, and he would kill me." So with eyes blinded with tears, and her heart filled with dread, she slipped out of the fire-lit hut, and vanished into the darkness of the forest as suddenly and silently as she had come.

Left alone, the Englishmen, cocking their guns and drawing their swords, awaited the coming of the foe. Presently eight or ten lusty fellows arrived, each bearing a great platter of food steaming hot and excellent to smell. They were very anxious that the Englishmen should at once lay aside their arms and sit down to supper. But Captain Smith would take no chances. Loaded gun in hand he stood over the messengers and made them taste each dish to be certain that none of them were poisoned. Having done this, he sent the men away. "And bid your master make haste," he said, "or we are ready for him."

Then the Englishmen sat down to supper; but they had no thought of sleep and all night long they kept watch.

Powhatan, too, kept watch, and every now and again he would send messengers to find out what the Englishmen were about. But each time they came, the Powhatans found the Englishmen on guard, so they dared not attack. At last day dawned, and with the rising tide the Englishmen sailed away, still to all seeming on friendly terms with the Powhatans.

Smith had now food enough to keep the colony from starvation for a short time at least. But his troubles were by no means over. The Indians were still often unfriendly, and the colonists themselves lazy and unruly. Some indeed worked well and cheerfully, but many wandered about idly, doing nothing.

At length it came about that thirty or forty men did all the work, the others being simply idle loiterers. Seeing this, Smith called all the colonists together one day and told them that he would suffer the idleness no longer. "Everyone must do his share," he said, "and he who will not work shall not eat." And so powerful had he grown that he was obeyed. The idle were forced to work, and soon houses were built and land cleared and tilled.

At length there seemed good hope that the colony would prosper. But now another misfortune befell it. For it was found that rats had got into the granaries and eaten nearly all the store of corn. So once again expeditions set forth to visit the Powhatans and gather more from them. But their supply, too, was running short; harvest was still a long way off, and all the colonists could collect was not enough to keep them from starvation. So seeing this Smith divided his men into companies, sending some down the river to fish, and others into the woods to gather roots and wild berries. But the lazy ones liked this little. They would have bartered away their tools and firearms for a few handfuls of meal rather than work so hard. They indeed became so mutinous that Smith hardly knew what to do with them. But at length he discovered the ringleader of these "gluttonous loiterers." Him he "worthily punished," and calling the others together, he told them very plainly that any man among them who did not do his share should be banished from the fort as a drone, till he mended his ways or starved.

To the idlers Smith seemed a cruel taskmaster; still they obeyed him. So the colony was held together, although in misery and hunger and without hope for the future.

At length one day to the men on the river there came a joyful sight. They saw a ship slowly sailing towards them. They could hardly believe their eyes, for no ship was expected; but they greeted it with all the more joy. It was a ship under Captain Samuel Argall, come, it is true, not to bring supplies, but to trade. Finding, however, that there was no hope of trade Captain Argall shared what food he had with the famished colonists, and so for a time rescued them from starvation. He also brought the news that more ships were setting out from home bringing both food and men.

In June 1609, this fleet of nine ships really did set out. But one ship was wrecked on the way, another, the *Sea Venture*, was cast ashore on the Bermudas; only seven arrived at length at Jamestown, bringing many new colonists. Unfortunately, among these new arrivals there were few likely to make good colonists. They were indeed for the most part wild, bad men whose friends had packed them off to that distant land in the hope of being rid of them forever. "They were," said one of the old colonists who wrote of them, "ten times more fit to spoil a Commonwealth than either to begin one or but help to maintain one."

Now with all these "unruly gallants" poured into his little commonwealth Smith found his position of President even more difficult than before. Still, for a time, if he could not keep them altogether in order, he at least kept them in check.

Then one day by a terrible accident his rule was brought to a sudden end. He was returning from an expedition up the James River when, through some carelessness, a bag of gunpowder in his boat was exploded. Smith was not killed by it, but he was sorely hurt. In great pain, and no longer able to think and act for others, he was carried back to Jamestown.

Here there was no doctor of any kind, and seeing himself then only a useless hulk, and in danger of death, Smith gave up his post, and leaving the colony, for which during two and a half years he had worked and thought and fought so hard, he sailed homeward.

Many of the unruly sort were glad to see him go, but his old companions with whom he had shared so many dangers and privations were filled with grief. "He hated baseness, sloth, pride, and indignity, more than any danger," it was said of him. "He never allowed more for himself than for his soldiers with him. Upon no danger would he send them where he would not lead them himself. He would never see us want what he either had or could by any means get us. He loved action more than words; and hated falsehood and covetousness worse than death."

So, loved and hated, but having all unknown to himself made a name which would live forever in the history of his land, the first great Virginian sailed from its shores. He returned no more. Some twenty years later he died in London and was buried in the church of St. Sepulchre there. Upon his tomb was carved a long epitaph telling of his valiant deeds. But in the great Fire of London the tomb was destroyed, and now no tablet marks the resting-place of the brave old pioneer.

Notes:

The word "ewer" refers to a wide-mouthed jug, used for washing.

This account and the quotes in it are taken from Captain John Smith's "The Generall Historie of Virginia."

Smith's command that "he who will not work shall not eat" comes from II Thessalonians 3:10, "For even when we were with you, this we commanded you, that if any would not work, neither should he eat."

Pronunciation Guide:

Werowocomoco – ware-oh-woe-COM-oh-coe

Chapter 15

How the Colony Was Saved

After Smith left, the colony of Jamestown fell into wild disorder. Everyone wanted to go his own way. A new President named Percy had indeed been chosen. But although an honest gentleman, he was sickly and weak and quite unfit to rule these turbulent spirits. So twenty or more would-be presidents soon sprang up, and in the whole colony there was neither obedience nor discipline.

No work was done, food was recklessly wasted, there was a drought, and very quickly famine stared the wretched colonists in the face. The terrible time afterwards known as the Starving Time had begun. When their stores were gone, the settlers tried to get more in the old way from the Powhatans. But they, seeing the miserable plight of the Englishmen, demanded guns and ammunition, swords and tools, for food.

And now there was no man among the colonists who knew how to manage the Powhatan Confederacy as Smith had managed it. There was no man among them who thought of the future. All they wanted was to stay for a time the awful pangs of hunger. So they bartered away their muskets and powder, their tools, and everything of value of which they were possessed. But even so the food the Native people gave them in return was not enough to keep body and soul together.

The colony became a place of horror, where pale skeleton-like creatures roamed about eyeing each other suspiciously, ready to kill each other for a crust or a bone. They quarreled among themselves, and they quarreled with the Powhatans. And the Powhatans, now no longer filled with awe, lay in wait for them and killed them almost without resistance if they ventured to crawl beyond the walls of the fort. Many more died of hunger and of disease brought on by hunger.

So less than eight months after Smith had sailed away, of the five hundred men he had left behind him but sixty remained alive. The colony was being wiped out, and the little town itself was disappearing; for the starving wretches had no strength or energy to fell trees and hew wood, and as soon as a man died his house was pulled down by his comrades and used as firewood. Already, too, weeds and briers overgrew the land which had been cleared for corn. Greater misery and desolation, it is hard to imagine. Yet the unhappy beings sank into a still deeper horror. Unable to relieve the pangs of hunger, they turned cannibal and fed upon each other. Thus the last depths of degradation were sounded, the last horrors of the Starving Time were reached.

Then at length one May day, two ships came sailing up the James River and anchored in the harbor. From their decks bronzed men in patched and ragged garments looked with astonished eyes upon the desolate scene.

These were the men of the wrecked *Sea Venture*, who had been cast ashore upon the Bermudas. Their ship had gone down, but they had been able to save both themselves and nearly everything out of her. Some of the best men of the expedition had sailed in the *Sea Venture*. Their leaders were brave and energetic; so instead of bemoaning their fate they had set to work with right good will, and after ten months' labor had succeeded in building two little ships which they named the *Patience* and the *Deliverance*. Then, having filled them with such stores as they could muster, they set sail joyfully to join their comrades at Jamestown. But now what horror and astonishment was theirs! They had hoped to find a flourishing town, surrounded by well-tilled fields. Instead they saw ruins and desolation. They had hoped to be greeted joyfully by stalwart, prosperous Englishmen. Instead a few gaunt, hollow-cheeked specters, who scarce seemed men, crawled to meet them.

Lost in amazement the newcomers landed, and as they listened to the tragic tale, pity filled their hearts. They gave the starving wretches food and comforted them as best they could. They had no great stores themselves, and they saw at once that with such scant supplies as they had it would be impossible to settle at Jamestown.

Even if they could get through the summer, the autumn would bring no relief, for the fields, where the corn for the winter's use should already have been sprouting, lay neglected and overgrown with weeds and briers. The houses where the newcomers might have lodged had disappeared. The very palisading which surrounded the settlement as a bulwark against the Powhatans had been pulled down for firewood. All the tools and implements which might have been used to rebuild the place had been bartered away to the Indians. The Powhatans themselves were no longer friendly, but hostile. Whichever way they looked, only misery and failure stared them in the face.

The Captains of the *Patience* and *Deliverance* talked long together, but even they could see no ray of hope. So with heavy hearts they resolved once more to abandon Virginia. They were loath indeed to come to this decision, loath indeed to own themselves defeated. But there seemed no other course left open to them.

So one day early in June, the pitiful remnant of the Jamestown Colony went on board the two waiting ships. Sir Thomas Gates, the brave and wise captain of the expedition, was the last to leave the ruined town. With backward looks he left it, and ere he weighed anchor he fired a last salute to the lost colony. Then the sails were set, and the two little ships drifted downstream towards the open sea, carrying the beaten settlers back to old England.

Another attempt to plant a New England beyond the seas had failed.

But next day as the little ships dropped downstream the sailors on the lookout saw a boat being rowed towards them. Was it a Native canoe? Did it come in peace or war? It drew nearer. Then it was seen that it was no Native canoe, but an English tugboat manned by English sailors. With a shout they hailed each other, and news was exchanged. Wonderful news it was to which the brokenhearted colonists listened.

Lord Delaware, the new Governor of Virginia, had arrived. His three good ships, well stored with food and all things necessary for the colony, were but a little way downstream. There was no need for the settlers to flee home to escape starvation and death.

It may be that to some this news was heavy news. It may be that some would gladly have turned their backs forever upon the spot where they had endured so much misery. But for the most part the colonists were unwilling to own defeat, and they resolved at once to return. So the ships were put about, and three days after they had left Jamestown, as they believed forever, the colonists once more landed there.

As Lord Delaware stepped on shore he fell upon his knees, giving thanks to God that he had come in time to save Virginia. After that the chaplain preached a sermon, then the new Governor, with all his company about him, read aloud the commission given to him by King James.

This was the first royal commission ever given to a governor of an English colony in America. In it Lord Delaware was given the power of life and death over "all and every such Person and Persons whatsoever...shall attempt to inhabit within the said several Precincts and Limits of the said Colony and Plantation." The colonists were, in fact, to be his subjects. And having read aloud his commission, and having thus as it were shown his authority, Lord Delaware next spoke sternly to his new subjects. He warned them that he would no longer endure their sluggish idleness or haughty disobedience. And if they did not amend their ways, they might look to it that the most severe punishment of the law would come upon them. Having thus spoken his mind plainly, to cheer them he told of the plentiful and good stores he had brought with him, of which all those who worked well and faithfully should have a share.

Now a new life began for the colony. All the settlers were made to work for some hours every day. Even the gentlemen among them, "whose breeding never knew what a day's labour meant," had to do their share. Soon the houses were rebuilt, the palisades stood again in place, two forts were erected to guard against attacks by the Native people, and at length the colony seemed to be on the fair way to success.

Of course, this did not all happen at once. The idlers were not easily turned into diligent workers, or unruly brawlers into peaceful citizens. Indeed it was only through most stern, and what would seem to us now most cruel punishments, that the unruly were forced to keep the law.

The winter after Lord Delaware came out as Governor, although not so hard as that of the Starving Time, was yet severe, and many of the colonists died. Lord Delaware, too, became so ill that in the spring he sailed home to England, and after a little time Sir Thomas Dale took his place as Deputy Governor.

Sir Thomas Dale was both a soldier and a statesman. He was full of energy and courage. Far-seeing and dogged, he was merciless to the evildoers, yet kindly to those who tried to do well. Under his stern yet righteous rule, the colony prospered.

At first only men settlers had come out, then one or two women joined them, and now many more women came, so that the men, instead of all living together, married and had homes of their own. Then, too, at first all a man's labor went into the common stock, and the men who worked little fared as well as those who worked a great deal. So the lazy fellow did as little as he could. "Glad was he could slip from his labor," says an old writer, "or slumber over his taske he cared not how."

Thus most of the work of the colony was left to the few who were industrious and willing. Sir Thomas Dale changed that. In return for a small yearly payment in corn he gave three acres of land to every man who wished it, for his own use. So, suddenly, a little community of farmers sprang up. Now that the land was really their own, to make of it what they would, each man tilled it eagerly, and soon such fine crops of grain were raised that the colony was no longer in dread of starvation. The settlers, too, began to spread and no longer kept within the palisade round Jamestown, "more especially as Jamestown," says an old writer, "was formerly scandaled for an unhealthfull aire." And here and there further up the river, little villages sprang up.

Since Smith had gone home, the Powhatans had remained unfriendly and a constant danger to the colonists. And now as they became thus scattered, the danger from the Powhatans became ever greater. Old Powhatan and his men were constantly making raids upon the Englishmen with whom he had once been so friendly. And in spite of the watch they kept, he often succeeded in killing them or taking them prisoner. He had also by now quite a store of swords, guns, and tools stolen from the English. And how to subdue him or force him to live on friendly terms with them once more, none knew.

Pocahontas, who had been so friendly and who had more than once saved the Englishmen from disaster, might have helped them. But she now never came near their settlement; indeed she seemed to have disappeared altogether. So the English could get no aid from her.

But now it happened one day that one of the adventurers, Samuel Argall, who was, according to John Smith, "a good Marriner, and a very civil gentleman," went sailing up the Appomattox in search of corn for the settlement. He had to go warily because no one could tell how the Powhatans would behave, for they would be friends or foes just as it suited them. If they got the chance of killing the Englishmen and stealing their goods they would do so. But if they were not strong enough to do that they would willingly trade for the colored cloths, beads and hatchets they so much wanted.

Presently Argall came to the country of Japazaws, one of the chiefs who was part of the Powhatan Confederacy. While here he was told that Pocahontas, the great Powhatan's daughter, was living with the Patawomeck tribe. As soon as he heard this, Captain Argall saw at once that here was a means of forcing the Powhatan tribe to make peace, and he resolved at all costs to get possession of Pocahontas. So sending for the chief he told him he must bring Pocahontas on board his ship.

But Japazaws was afraid and refused to do this.

"Then we are no longer brothers and friends," said Argall.

"My father," said the chief, "be not wroth. For if I do this thing the Powhatan will make war upon me and upon my people."

"My brother," said Argall, "have no fear; if so be that the Powhatan shall make war upon you I will join with you against him to overthrow him utterly. I mean, moreover, no manner of hurt to Pocahontas, but will only keep her as hostage until peace be made between the Powhatan and the Englishmen. If therefore you do my bidding, I will give to you the copper kettle which you desire so much."

Now Japazaws longed greatly to possess the copper kettle. So he promised to do as Argall asked, and began to cast about for an excuse for getting Pocahontas on board. Soon he fell upon a plan. He bade his wife pretend that she was very anxious to see the Englishman's ship. But when she asked to be taken on board, he refused to go with her. Again and again she asked. Again and again Japazaws refused. Then the poor lady wept with disappointment and at length the chief, pretending to be very angry, swore that he would beat her if she did not cease her asking and her tears. But as she still begged and wept, he said he would take her if Pocahontas would go, too.

To please the old woman, Pocahontas went. Captain Argall received all three very courteously and made a great feast for them in his cabin. Japazaws, however, was so eager to get his promised kettle that he could little enjoy the feast but kept kicking Captain Argall under the table as much as to say, "I have done my part, now you do yours."

At length Captain Argall told Pocahontas that she must stay with him until peace was made between her father and the Englishmen. As soon as the old chief and his wife heard that they began to howl, and cry, and make a great noise, so as to pretend that they knew nothing about the plot. Pocahontas, too, began to cry. But Argall assured her that no harm was intended her, and that she need have no fear. So she was soon comforted and dried her eyes.

As for Japazaws and his wife, they were made quite happy with the copper kettle and a few other trifles, and went merrily back to the shore.

A messenger was then sent to the Powhatan telling him that his daughter, whom he loved so dearly, was a prisoner, and that he could only ransom her by sending back all the Englishmen he held prisoner, with all their guns, swords and tools which he had stolen.

When Powhatan got this news, he was both angry and sorry. For he loved his daughter very dearly, but he loved the Englishmen's tools and weapons almost more. He did not know what to do, so for three months he did nothing. Then at last he sent back seven of his prisoners, each one carrying a useless gun.

"Tell your chieftain," he said, "that all the rest of the arms of the Englishmen are lost, or have been stolen from me. But if the Englishmen will give back my daughter I will give satisfaction for all the other things I have taken, together with five hundred bushels of corn, and will make peace forever."

But the Englishmen were not easily deceived. They returned a message to the chief saying, "Your daughter is well used. But we do not believe the rest of our arms are either lost or stolen, and therefore until you send them, we will keep your daughter."

Powhatan was so angry when he got this message that for a long time, he would have no further dealings with the Englishmen but continued to vex and harass them as much as he could.

At length Sir Thomas Dale, seeking to put an end to this, took Pocahontas, and with a hundred and fifty men sailed up the river to the Powhatan's chief town.

As soon as the Powhatans saw the Englishmen, they came down to the river's bank, jeering at them and insulting them, haughtily demanding why they had come.

"We have brought the Powhatan's daughter," replied the Englishmen. "For we are come to receive the ransom promised, and if you do not give it willingly, we will take it by force."

But the Powhatans were not in the least afraid of that threat. They jeered the more.

"If so be," they cried, "that you are come to fight you are right welcome, for we are ready for you. But we advise you, if you love your lives, to retire with haste. Else we will serve you as we have served others of your countrymen."

"Oh," answered the Englishmen, "we must have a better answer than that," and driving their ship nearer to the shore they made ready to land.

But as soon as they were within bowshot, the Powhatans let fly their arrows. Thick and fast they fell, rattling on the deck, glancing from the men's armor, wounding not a few. This reception made the

Englishmen angry, so without more ado they launched their boats and made for the shore. The Powhatans fled at their coming, and so enraged were the colonists against them that they burned their houses and utterly destroyed their town. Then they sailed on up the river in pursuit of the Powhatans.

Next day they came up again with the Powhatans. They were now not so insolent and sent a messenger to ask why the Englishmen had burned their town.

"Why did you fire upon us?" asked the Englishmen, sternly.

"Brothers," replied the men, "we did not fire upon you. It was but some others who did so. We intend you no hurt and are your friends."

With these and many other fair words they tried to pacify the Englishmen. So the Englishmen made peace with them. Then the warriors sent a messenger to Powhatan who was a day's journey off; and the Englishmen were told they must wait two days for his answer.

Meanwhile the Englishmen asked to see their comrades whom the Powhatans had taken prisoner.

"We cannot show them to you," they replied, "for they have all run away in fear lest you should hang them. But Powhatan's men are pursuing after them and will doubtless bring them back."

"Then where are the swords and guns which you have stolen from us?" demanded the Englishmen.

"These you shall have tomorrow," replied the Powhatans.

But, as the Englishmen well knew, this was all idle talk and deceit, and next day no message came from Powhatan, neither were any swords nor guns forthcoming. So once more the Englishmen set sail and went still further up the river.

Here quite close to another village belonging to the Powhatans they came upon four hundred men in war paint. When they saw the Englishmen, the Powhatans yelled and danced and dared them to come ashore. This the Englishmen, nothing daunted, accordingly did. The Powhatans on their side showed no fear, but walked boldly up and down among the Englishmen, demanding to speak with their captain.

So the chiefs were brought to Sir Thomas.

"Why do you come against us thus?" they asked. "We are friends and brothers. Let us not fight until we have sent once again to our King to know his pleasure. Then if he sends not back the message of peace, we will fight you and defend our own as best we may."

The Englishmen knew well that by all this talk of peace the Powhatans wanted but to gain time so that they might be able to carry away and hide their stores. Still they had no desire to fight if by any other means they might gain their end. So they promised a truce until noon the day following. "And if we then decide to fight you, you shall be warned of it by the sounding of our drums and trumpets," they said.

The truce being settled Pocahontas' two brothers came on board the Englishmen's ships to visit their sister. And when they saw that she was well cared for and appeared to be quite happy, they were very glad, for they had heard that she was ill-treated and most miserable. But finding her happy they promised to persuade their father to ransom her and make friends again with the Englishmen.

Seeing them thus friendly, Sir Thomas suggested that Pocahontas' two brothers should stay on board his vessel as hostages while he sent two of his company to parley with Powhatan. This was accordingly done, and Master John Rolfe and Master Sparkes set off on their mission. When, however, they reached the village where Powhatan was hiding, they found him still in high dudgeon, and he refused to see them, or speak with them. So they had to be content with seeing his brother, who treated them with all courtesy and kindness and promised to do his best to pacify Powhatan.

It was now April, and high time for the colonists to be back on their farms sowing their corn. So with this promise they were fain to be content in the meantime. And having agreed upon a truce until harvest time they set sail once more for Jamestown, taking Pocahontas with them.

One at least among the company of Englishmen was glad that the negotiations with Powhatan had come to nothing, and that Pocahontas had not been ransomed. That was Master John Rolfe. For Pocahontas was beautiful and kind, and John Rolfe had fallen madly in love with her. So he had no desire that she should return to her own tribe, but rather that she should return to Jamestown and marry him.

Pocahontas, too, was quite fond of John Rolfe, although she had never forgotten her affection for the great captain whose life she had saved. The Englishmen, however, told her that he had gone away never to come back anymore, and that very likely he was dead. Pocahontas was then easily persuaded to marry John Rolfe. But he himself, although he loved her very much, had some misgivings. For was this beautiful woman not a heathen?

That difficulty was, however, soon overcome. For Pocahontas made no objection to becoming a Christian. So one day there was a great gathering in the little church at Jamestown when the heathen princess stood beside the fort, and the water of Christian baptism was sprinkled on her face, and she was given the Bible name of Rebecca.

And now when Powhatan heard that his daughter was going to marry one of the Englishmen, he was quite pleased. He forgot all his anger, sent many of his men to be present at the wedding, and swore to be the friend and brother of the Englishmen forever more.

Sir Thomas Dale was delighted. So everyone was pleased, and one morning early in April four hundred years ago all the inhabitants of the country round, both Powhatans and Englishmen, gathered to see the wedding. And from that day for eight years, for as long as the Powhatan lived, there was peace between him and his brothers, the Englishmen.

Notes:

Lord Delaware's commission quote is taken from the Second Charter of Virginia, May 23, 1609.

"Whose breeding never knew" (the quote of Lord Delaware) is from a communication dated July 7, 1610, quoted in Edward Duffield Neill's The English Colonization of American During the Seventeenth Century, *1871.*

"Glad was he could slip from his labor" is taken from The Complete Works of Captain John Smith, *1580-1631.*

The quote about "unhealthfull aire" can be found in Generall historie of Virginia *by Captain John Smith.*

Japazaws was also called Iopassus, chief of the town of Passapatanzy.

After what some historians call the First Anglo-Powhatan War (1609-1614), there came a time of peace. It was called "The Peace of Pocahontas," since it began with her marriage to John Rolfe and led to a cessation of the conflict between the English colonists and the Powhatans. That peace would last eight years.

Pronunciation Guide:

Argall – AR-gull

Japazaws – JAP-uh-zaws

Patawomeck – Puh-TOW-wuh-meck. It was from this pronunciation that the English called the river the Potomac.

Chapter 16

How Pocahontas Took a Journey Over the Seas

At peace with the Powhatans, the colonists could till their fields without fear of attack. And now, besides corn, they began to grow tobacco.

You remember that Columbus had noticed how the Indians of his "India" smoked rolled-up dried leaves. But no one paid much attention to it. Then the men of Raleigh's expedition again noticed it. They tried it themselves, found it comforting, and brought both tobacco and the habit home with them. And soon not only the seafaring adventurers, but many a man who was never likely to see the ocean or adventure beyond his hometown, had taken to smoking. That, too, despite his king's disgust at it. For James thought smoking was "a custom loathsome to the eye, hateful to the nose, harmful to the brain, dangerous to the lungs, and in the black stinking fume thereof, nearest resembling the horrible Stygian smoke of the pit that is bottomless." He indeed wrote a little book against it, which he called "*A Counterblaste to Tobacco.*" But no one paid much attention to him. The demand for tobacco became greater and greater, and soon the Virginian farmers found that there was a sale for as much tobacco as they could grow, and that a crop of it paid better than anything else.

Up till now the colony had been a constant disappointment to the "adventurers" - that is, to the people who had given the money to fit out the expeditions - the "shareholders," we would now call them.

Most of them had adventured their money, not with any idea of founding a New England beyond the seas where men should settle down as farmers and tillers of the soil. They had adventured it rather for the finding of gold and pearls, jewels and spices, so that it might be repaid quickly, and a hundredfold. But year by year passed, and all these glittering hopes were doomed to disappointment. No gold was found. The adventurers saw their money being swallowed up for nought. They grew discontented and grumbled, some of them refused to pay any more, refused to throw more away on an empty dream. They little knew that they were helping to found a new State which in time was to become one of the world's greatest powers. They little knew that in days to come their money should produce a harvest a thousand, thousandfold, and that from the broad land, of which they had helped to settle a tiny corner, was to come wealth such as in their wildest imaginings, they had never dreamt.

Meanwhile, anything a Virginian wanted he could buy with tobacco. Indeed, after a time the Virginians threw themselves with such complete enthusiasm into the growing of tobacco that they were reproached for neglecting everything else because of it.

The English were not the only people who had set forth to find golden wealth and broad lands beyond the seas. Both the French and the Dutch had carried their standard across the ocean and planted it upon the further shores. Already, too, the struggle for possession began.

Captain Argall, in one of his many expeditions, sailing northward to the Bay of Fundy, found a French Jesuit colony settled there in Acadia. Argall swooped down upon them, and claiming the whole continent by right of Cabot's discovery, he utterly destroyed the colony, burning the houses to the ground, killing missionaries, taking prisoners, and carrying off the cattle.

Argall next found a Dutch colony on the Hudson River, on "Manhatas Isle." Here he contented himself with ordering the Governor to pull down the Dutch flag and run up the English one. To save his colony, the Dutchman did as he was commanded. But as soon as the arrogant Englishman was out of sight, he calmly ran up his own flag once more.

Meanwhile under Sir Thomas Dale, Virginia continued to prosper. Then after five years' rule, Sir Thomas went home, and the colony was left to a new ruler. With him went John Rolfe and his wife Pocahontas, together with their little baby son.

Now began a wonderful new life for the beautiful young woman. Only a few years before she had been a merry, little, carefree girl, turning cartwheels all over the Jamestown fort, and playing with the boys and girls. Now she found herself treated as a great lady.

In those days, the people in England had very little idea of the life out in the new world. Powhatan, they had heard, was a king, a sort of emperor, indeed, and they doubtless pictured him as living in a stately palace, wearing a golden crown and velvet robes. That a king should be living in a bark hut, wearing a crown of feathers on his head, a string of beads about his neck, and a deerskin around his waist, they could not imagine. As the Powhatan was a king, then his daughter was a princess, and as such must be treated with all respect.

It is even said that John Rolfe was roundly scolded by King James for daring to marry a princess without first asking leave.

"For," he gravely pointed out, "if the Powhatan was a king and Pocahontas his daughter, when the Powhatan died, Rolfe or his baby son might become King of Virginia. It was not meet or right that a commoner should thus lightly take upon himself to marry the daughter of a brother sovereign."

Everyone, then, was ready to treat Pocahontas with deference. Besides this, John Smith wrote to the Queen relating all that she had done for the Colony of Virginia and begging her to be kind to the Native girl who had done so much for England. For that or some other reason the Queen took an interest in the little princess. Pocahontas was presented to her and was often seen at the theater or other entertainment with her. The ladies of the court were made to treat Pocahontas with great ceremony. They addressed her as "Princess" or "Lady," remained standing before her, and walked backwards when they left her presence; famous artists painted her portrait; poets wrote of her, and in one of his plays, Ben Jonson calls her

> "The Blessed
> Pokahontas (as the historian calls her)
> And great king's daughter of Virginia."

In fact, she became the rage. She was the talk of the town. Even coffee-houses and taverns were named after her: La Belle Sauvage (*the beautiful savage*). And it is interesting to remember that a great publishing house in London takes its name from one of these old taverns. Books go out to all the world from the sign of La Belle Sauvage, thus forming a link between the present and that half-forgotten American "princess" of so long ago.

In spite of all the homage and flattery poured upon her, Pocahontas yet remained modest and simple, enchanting all who met her. And among all the new delights of England, she had the joy of seeing once again the great Chief she had loved and called her father in days gone by.

Her joy was all the greater because she had believed him to be dead. When Smith first came to see her, her feelings were so deep that at first she could not speak. She greeted him in silence, then suddenly turning away, she hid her face and wept. But after a little she recovered herself, and began to speak of the old days, and of how she had thought he was dead. "I knew no other," she said, "until I came to Plymouth."

In many ways Pocahontas showed her joy at again recovering her old friend. But when she found that Smith was not going to treat her as an old friend, but as if she were a great lady, and call her Princess like all the others round her, she was hurt.

"You did promise the Powhatan that what was yours should be his, and he the like to you," she said. "You called him father being in his land a stranger, and by the same reason, so must I do you."

"Lady," replied Smith, "I dare not allow that title, for you are a King's daughter."

But from the man who had known her in those strange, wild days in far-off Virginia, from the man she had looked upon as a great and powerful chief, Pocahontas would have no such nonsense. She laughed at him.

"Were you not afraid," she said defiantly, "to come into my father's countrie, and caused feare in him and all his people (but mee) and feare you here I should call you father? I tell you then I will, and you shall calle me childe, and so I will bee for ever and ever your Countrieman."

Pocahontas also challenged John Smith. "They did tell us always you were dead, and I knew no other till I came to Plimoth; yet Powhatan did command Uttamatomakkin to seeke you, and know the truth, because your Countriemen will lie much."

Pocahontas took all the strangeness of her new surroundings very simply. But some of her attendants were utterly overwhelmed with wonder and awe at the things they saw. Uttamatomakkin, in particular, who was accounted a very clever man among his own tribe, had been sent by Powhatan to take particular note of everything in England. Among other things, he had been charged to count the people. So on landing at Plymouth, he provided himself with a long stick and proceeded to make a notch in it for every man he met. But he met so many people that he could not make notches fast enough; so in a very short time he grew weary of that and threw his stick away.

Coming to London he was more amazed than ever. Never had he seen so great a city nor so many folk all gathered together, and among them not one familiar face. So he welcomed Captain John Smith like an old friend, and eagerly questioned him as to the wonders of this strange country. More especially he asked to see God, the King and Queen, and the Prince.

Captain Smith tried as best he could to explain to the poor man about God, telling him He could not be seen. As, to the King, he added, "you have seen him."

"No," said the man, "I have not seen your great King."

Then when Captain Smith explained that the little man with a jeweled feather in his cap and sword by his side, who had one day spoken to him was the King, Uttamatomakkin was much disappointed.

"You gave Powhatan a white Dog," he said, "which Powhatan fed as himselfe. But your King gave me nothing, and I am better than your white Dog."

However, if Uttamatomakkin was disappointed with the manner in which the King had received him, he was much made of by others. For everyone was eager to see him.

Pocahontas loved England where she was so kindly treated. She took to the new life so well that John Smith wrote to Queen Anne that Pocahontas "became very formal and civil after our English manner." But she who had been used to roam the wild woods could not live in the confinement of towns, and soon she became very ill. So she made up her mind at length, sorely against her will, to go back to Virginia with her husband and little boy. Captain Argall was about to return there as Deputy Governor. So Pocahontas and her husband took passages in his boat.

But Pocahontas was never again to see her native shore. She went on board Captain Argall's boat, the *George,* and indeed set sail from London, but before she reached Gravesend, she became so ill that she had to be taken ashore, and there she died. She was buried in the chancel of the Parish Church. Later the Church was burned down, but it was rebuilt, and as a memorial to Pocahontas, American ladies have placed a stained-glass window there, as well as a pulpit made of Virginian wood.

John Rolfe returned alone to Virginia, leaving his little son Thomas behind him in the care of an uncle. Thomas remained in England until he was grown up, and then went to his native land. There he married, and had a daughter, and became the ancestor of several Virginian families who are to this day proud to trace their descent from beautiful Pocahontas and her English husband.

Notes:

King James I's pamphlet against tobacco was published in 1604.

Jesuits were an order of Catholic priests that did missionary work. The order was founded by St. Ignatius Loyola in 1534.

King James' scolding of John Rolfe for marrying a princess without his permission is taken from the writing of Robert Beverley, Jr., a historian of early colonial Virginia.

"The blessed Pokahontas" is from Ben Jonson's play **The Staple of News,** Act II.

Uttamatomakkin is also known as Tomocomo.

Quotes from John Smith and Pocahontas' encounter in England and Uttamakomakkin's experiences are taken from John Smith's **Generall** **Historie of Virginia, New-England and the Summer Isles,** *1624.*

Pronunciation Guide:

Uttamatomakkim – oo-tuh-MOT-uh-mok-in

Chapter 17

A Year to be Remembered, and the Peace of Pocahontas Ends

The Colony of Virginia which had prospered so greatly under Sir Thomas Dale had fallen again on evil days. For Samuel Argall, who now governed, proved a tyrant. Dale had been autocratic, but he had been autocratic for the good of the colony. Argall was autocratic for his own gains. He extorted money and tribute from the colonists to make himself rich, and profits which should have gone to the company went into his pocket. Again and again the colonists sent home complaints of Argall's doings. At length, these complaints became so loud and long that the company once more sent Lord Delaware out as Governor.

But on the way Lord Delaware died, and the party of settlers he was bringing out arrived without him. On their arrival Argall at once took possession of Lord Delaware's private papers, and much to his disgust he found among them one telling Lord Delaware to arrest Argall and send him back to England.

This made Argall very angry; it also made him more despotic and cruel than ever. In consequence still more bitter complaints reached home from the colonists.

At this time, the company at home were quarrelling among themselves. But in the end, they sent out a new Governor called Sir George Yeardley. He, too, had orders to arrest Argall and send him home. But Argall somehow came to know of it, and he made up his mind not to go home a prisoner. So before the new Governor could arrive he packed up his goods, and leaving the colony to take care of itself, sailed off to England.

The Virginians now were heartily tired of despots and thought that it was time that they had some say in the matter of governing themselves. At the head of the company at home there was at this time a wise man named Sandys. He also thought that it would be best for the colony to be self-governing.

And so on July 30th, 1619, the first General Election was held in Virginia, and the first Parliament of Englishmen in America met. There were by this time about two thousand people living in the colony, and the settlements were scattered about on both sides of the river for sixty miles or so above Jamestown. So the colony was divided into eleven parts or constituencies, each constituency sending two members to the little parliament. These members were called burgesses, and the parliament was called the House of Burgesses. But there was no special building in which the burgesses could gather, so the meetings were held in the little wooden church at Jamestown. And thus with such small beginnings were the first foundations of a free and independent nation laid. And because of the founding of this House of Burgesses, 1619 stands out as the year most to be remembered in all the early days of Virginia.

But 1619 has to be remembered for another, and this time a sad reason: for it saw not only the beginnings of freedom, but it marked the beginnings of slavery in the Virginia colony.

Just a month after the opening of the House of Burgesses, a Dutch vessel anchored at Jamestown, at a place called Point Comfort.

Prior to this, Portuguese and African raiders captured many Angolans during a war. The captives were marched to the capital city and forced onto ships. During the Atlantic crossing, many died from the harsh conditions. One Portuguese ship was later attacked by a Dutch ship, the *White Lion*, and twenty of the Angolans were taken. The *White Lion* landed at Point Comfort, and all the Angolans on board were sold, in exchange for food. And thus slavery was first introduced upon the Virginian plantations.

In 1619, too, there arrived the first shipload of women colonists. Nearly all the settlers were men. A few indeed had brought their wives and daughters with them, but for the most part the colony was a community of men. Among these there were many who were young, and as they grew rich and prosperous, they wanted to marry and have homes of their own. But there was no one for them to marry. So at length someone at home fell upon the plan of persuading young women to go out to Virginia to settle there, and in 1619 a shipload of ninety came out. As soon as they arrived, they found many young men eager to marry them, and sometimes they must have found it difficult to make a choice. But as soon as a young man was accepted, he had to pay the Company 120 lbs., afterwards raised to 150 lbs., of tobacco as the price of his bride's passage across the seas. Then they were free to marry as soon as they pleased.

After this from time to time, women went out to the colony. Sometimes we read of "one widow and eleven maids," or again of "fifty maids for wives." And always there came with them a letter from the company at home to the old men of the colony reminding them that these young women did not come to be servants. "We pray you therefore to be fathers to them in their business, not enforcing them to marry against their wills, neither send we them to be servants," they wrote. And if the girls did not marry at once they were to be treated as guests and "put to several householders that have wives till they can be provided of husbands."

Helped in this quaint fashion and in others, the colony prospered and grew ever larger. It would have prospered even more had it not been for the outbreak of a kind of plague, which the colonists simply called "the sickness." It attacked chiefly the new settlers and was so deadly that in one year a thousand of them died. Doctors were not very skillful in those days, and although they did their best, all their efforts were of little use, till at length the dread disease wore itself out.

But in spite of all difficulties the colony grew, the settlements extended farther and farther in a long line up and down both banks of the James from Chesapeake Bay to what is now Richmond. Had the Native people been unfriendly, the colony could not have stretched out in this fashion without great danger to the settlers. Ever since the marriage of Pocahontas to John Rolfe in 1614, the Powhatan Confederacy had been at peace with the Englishmen, and the settlers had lost all fear of attack from them. The Powhatans, indeed, might be seen wandering freely about the towns and farms. They came into the houses, and even shared the meals of the farmer and his household. Nothing, to all outward seeming, could be more friendly than the relations between the Powhatans and the Englishmen.

Then old Powhatan, the father of Pocahontas, died, and his brother Opechancaneough became chief of the tribe. It was he who first had captured Captain John Smith and brought him to Werocomoco. So the Governor took the precaution of sending a messenger to him with renewed expressions of friendship.

Opechancaneough received the messenger kindly and sent him back to his master. "Tell your leader," he said, "that I hold the peace so sure that the skies shall fall sooner than it should be broken."

But at this very time, he and his people were plotting utterly to destroy the settlers. Yet they gave no hint of it. They had planned a general massacre, yet two days before the 22nd of March, 1622, the day fixed for it, some settlers were safely guided through the woods by the Powhatans. They came as usual, quite unarmed, into the settlers' houses, selling game, fish, and furs in exchange for glass beads and such trifles. Even on the night of the 21st of March, they borrowed the settlers' boats so that many of their tribe could get quickly across the river. The next morning in many places the Powhatans were sitting at breakfast with the settlers and their families when suddenly, as at a given signal, they sprang up, and, seizing the settlers' own weapons, killed them all, sparing neither men, women, nor children. So sudden was the onslaught that many a man fell dead without a cry, seeing not the hand which smote him. In the workshops, in the fields, in the gardens, wherever they were, wherever their daily work took them, they were thus suddenly and awfully struck down.

For days and weeks, the Powhatans had watched the habits of the settlers until they knew the daily haunts of every man. Then they had planned one swift and deadly blow which was to wipe out the whole colony. And so cunning was their plot, so complete and perfect their treachery, that they might have succeeded but for the love of one faithful young Native named Chanco. This young man, newly converted to Christianity and belonging to a man named Perry, lived with one of the settlers named Pace. But Pace treated him more as a son than as a servant, and Chanco had become very devoted to him. When, then, Chanco was told that his chief commanded him to murder his master, he felt that he could not do it. Instead, he went at once to Pace and told him of the plot. Pace then made ready to defend himself and sent warnings to all the other settlers within reach. Thus a great many of the colonists were saved from death, but three hundred and forty-seven Englishmen were cruelly slain.

This sudden and treacherous attack, after so many years of peace, enraged the settlers, and they followed the Powhatans with a terrible vengeance. They hunted them like wild beasts, tracking them down with bloodhounds, driving them mercilessly from place to place, until, their corn destroyed, their houses burned, their canoes smashed to splinters, and hundreds killed in retaliation, the Powhatans were fain to sue for mercy, and peace once more was restored for more than twenty years.

Notes:

As Dana Huntley writes in **America's Forgotten Colonial History,** *"The first black Africans brought to Jamestown came on a Dutch ship as indentured servants in 1619. Within a generation, they did not get out of their indenture, and race slavery became hereditary." (Lyons Press, 2019, p. 143)*

While 1619 has come to be a symbolic date, slavery has existed for millennia before this, and enslaved Africans were in the colonies prior to that time. Author Michael Guasco writes in an article for history. com, "To ignore what had been happening with relative frequency in the broader Atlantic world over the preceding 100 years or so understates the real brutality of the ongoing slave trade, of which the 1619 group were undoubtedly a part, and minimizes the significant African presence in the Atlantic world to that point." https://www.history.com/.amp/news/

american-slavery-before-jamestown-1619 It was in 1705 that slavery was codified in law through the passage of the Virginia Slave Codes.

John Rolfe's letter to Sir Edwin Sandys said, "About the latter end of August, a Dutch man of Warr of the burden of a 160 tunnes arrived at Point-Comfort, the Comandors name Capt Jope, his Pilott for the West Indies one Mr Marmaduke an Englishman. They mett with the Treasurer in the West Indyes, and determyned to hold consort shipp hetherward, but in their passage lost one the other. He brought not any thing but 20. and odd Negroes, which the Governor and Cape Marchant bought for victualls (whereof he was in greate need as he pretended) at the best and easyest rates they could." From **The Records of the Virginia Company of London, Volume III,** *p. 243.*

Quotes about women brought to be brides are taken from **The Records of the Virginia Company of London, Volume III,** *pp. 256-257.*

Some historians speculate that Opechancaneough was the same person as Paquiquineo (also known as Don Luis de Velasco), a close relative of Powhatan who was captured by a Spanish expedition in 1561 and taken to Spain, Cuba, and Mexico. He returned to Virginia in 1571 as an interpreter for Jesuit missionaries and was involved in a massacre of them there.

This attack on March 22nd started what has been called the Second Anglo-Powhatan War (1622-1632).

Pronunciation Guide:

Opechancaneough – OPE-uh-CAN-kun-oe

Chapter 18

How Englishmen Fought a Duel With Tyranny

At last Virginia prospered. But while it prospered, the man who had first conceived the idea of this New England beyond the seas had fallen on evil days. Sir Walter Raleigh had been thrown into prison by King James. There for twelve long years he languished, only to be set free at length on condition that he should find a gold mine for his King. He failed to find the mine, and by his efforts only succeeded in rousing to greater heights than before the Spanish hatred against him. For Spain claimed the land and gold of which Raleigh had gone in search. And now the King of Spain demanded that he should be punished. And James, weakly yielding to his outcry, condemned Sir Walter to death. So on 29th of October, 1618, this great pioneer laid his head upon the block, meeting death as gallantly as ever man died.

"I shall yet live to see it an English nation," he had said of Virginia, after his own fifth failure to found a colony, and his words had come true. But long ere his death Raleigh had ceased to have any connection with Virginia. And perhaps there was scarce a man among those who had made their homes there who remembered that it was Raleigh who had prepared the way, that but for Raleigh a new Spain and not a New England might have been planted on the American shores.

So the death of Raleigh made no difference to the fortunes of Virginia. But the same stupidity, that same "wonderful instinct for the wrong side of every question" which made James kill his great subject, also made him try to stifle the infant colony. So while in

151

spite of sickness and massacre the colony prospered, the company at home was passing through strenuous times. The head or treasurer of the company was still that Sir Edwin Sandys who had been the chief mover in giving the colony self-government. King James, who was full of great ideas about the divine right of kings, had never forgiven him that. He was as eager as any of his people to build up a colonial Empire, but he desired that it should be one which should be dependent on himself. He had no intention of allowing colonies to set themselves up against him.

Now the time came to elect a new treasurer, and the company being very pleased with Sandys, decided to elect him again. But when King James heard that, he was very angry. He called the company a school of treason and Sandys his greatest enemy. Then, flinging himself out of the room in a terrible passion, he shouted "Choose the Devil if you will, but not Sir Edwin Sandys."

Still in spite of the King's anger, the company decided to go its own way. They had their charter sealed with the King's seal, signed with the King's name, which gave them the right of freely electing their own officers, and not even the King should be allowed to interfere with that right.

On the day of the election, nearly five hundred of the "adventurers" gathered together. Three names were put up for election, Sir Edwin's heading the list. But just as the voting was about to begin, a messenger from the King arrived.

"It is not the King's pleasure that Sir Edward Sandys should be chosen," he said, "so he has sent to you a list of four, one of which you may choose."

At this, dead silence fell upon the company, every man lost in amazement at this breach of their charter. For minutes the heavy silence lasted. Then there arose murmurs which grew ever louder, until amid cries of anger it was proposed to turn the King's messengers out.

"No," said the Earl of Southampton, "let the noble gentlemen keep their places. Let them stay and see that we do everything in a manner which is fair and above board. For this business is of so great concernment that it can never be too solemnly, too thoroughly or too publicly examined."

Others agreed that this was right. So the messengers stayed. Then there came impatient cries from every part of the hall, "The Charter! The Charter! God save the King!"

So the charter was brought and solemnly read.

Then the secretary stood up. "I pray you, gentlemen," he said, "to observe well the words of the charter on the point of electing a Governor. You see it is thereby left to your own free choice. This I take it is so very plain that we shall not need to say anything more about it. And no doubt these gentlemen when they depart will give his Majesty a just information of the case."

This speech was received with great noise and cheering. In the midst of it, a friend of Sir Edwin's stood up and begged for silence. And when the noise had abated a little, he said, "Sir Edwin asks me to say that he withdraws his name for election. I therefore propose that the King's messengers choose two names and that we choose a third. Then let all these three names be set upon the balloting box. And so go to the election in God's name. And let His will be done."

Thereupon with one voice the whole assembly cried out, "Southampton! Southampton!"

The King's messengers then pretended that they were quite pleased. "The King," they said, "had no desire to infringe their rights. He desired no more than that Sir Edwin Sandys should not be chosen."

Then they named two from the King's list, and the ballot was immediately taken; the result being that one of the King's men had two votes, the other but one, and the Earl of Southampton all the rest.

When the King heard of this result, he was a little anxious and apologetic. The messengers, he said, had mistaken his intention. He had only meant to recommend his friends, and not to forbid the company to elect any other. But once again Englishmen had fought a duel with tyranny and won.

From this day, however, the King's hatred of the company became deadly. He harassed it in every way and at last in 1624 took its charter away and made Virginia a Crown Colony. Henceforth, in theory at least, self-government was taken away from Virginia, and to the King alone belonged the right of appointing the Governor and Council. But in fact, the change made little difference to the colony. For in the spring of 1625 King James died, and his son Charles I, who succeeded him upon the throne, had so much else to trouble him that he paid little heed to Virginia.

Note:

"Adventurers" was a term that referred to both investors and settlers in the Virginia Company of London, and it came from James I's royal charter of 1606.

Pronunciation Guide:

Sandys - SANDZ

Chapter 19

The Coming of the Cavaliers

With a new King on the throne, life in Virginia went on much as it had done. Governors came and went, were good or bad, strong or weak. There were troubles with the Native people, and troubles at home about the sale of tobacco; still the colony lived and prospered. The early days of struggle were over.

Virginia now was no longer looked upon as a place of exile where with luck one could make a fortune and return home to England to enjoy it. Men now began to find Virginia a pleasant place, and to look upon it as their home. The great woods were full of game, the streams were full of fish, so that the Englishman could shoot and angle to his heart's content. The land was so fertile that he did not need to work half so hard to earn a living as he had to do at home, while the climate was far kindlier.

So the colony prospered. And it was to this prosperous colony that in 1642 Sir William Berkeley was appointed Governor. He was a courtly, hot-tempered, imperious gentleman, a thorough cavalier who dressed in satin and lace and at times ruled like a tyrant. Berkeley spent a good deal of time persecuting the Puritans who had found refuge in Virginia.

For just about the time of Berkeley's appointment, a fierce religious war between Cavalier and Puritan was beginning in England, and already some Puritans had fled to Virginia to escape persecution at home. But Berkeley soon showed them that they had come to the wrong place and bade them "depart the Colony with all convenience."

Berkeley did not believe in freedom of thought, and he disapproved just as much of education, for that had encouraged freedom of thought. "I thank God," he said some years later, "there are no free schools in Virginia or printing, and I hope we shall not have them these hundred years. For learning has brought disobedience and heresy, and sects into the world, and printing has divulged them, and libels against the best government. God keep us from both."

In England the quarrel between King and people grew ever fiercer and more bitter. Virginia so far away heard the echo of it, and there, as in England, men took sides. The men in Virginia were ready enough to stand up to the King and speak their mind when he threatened their liberties. But when they heard that the people in England had taken the King prisoner and were talking of beheading him, they were horrified. To lay bands upon his person, to lead him to the block, to take his life! That seemed to them very terrible. And when at length the news of the King's death reached Virginia, the Virginians forgot their grievances, they became King's men. And Berkeley, a fervent Royalist, wrote to his brother Royalists at home asking them to come out to Virginia, there to find new homes far from the rule of the hated "usurper" Oliver Cromwell.

Many came, fleeing from their native land "in horror and despairs at the bloody and bitter stroke." Before the year was out, at least a thousand Cavaliers had found a home in Virginia. They were kindly, even affectionately, received. Every house was open to them, every hand stretched out to help.

In October the House of Burgesses met and at once declared that the beheading of "the late most excellent and now undoubtedly sainted King" was treason. And if anyone in Virginia dared to defend "the late traitorous proceedings against the aforesaid King of most happy memory," they, too, would be found guilty of treason and worthy of death. Worthy of death, too, should be anyone who seemed by word or deed to doubt the right of "His Most Sacred Majesty that now is" to the Colony of Virginia. Thus Charles II, a homeless wanderer, was acknowledged King of Virginia.

In this manner did little Virginia fling down the gauntlet to Great Britain. It was a daring deed, and one not likely to go unheeded by the watchful Cromwell. Yet two years and more passed. Then British ships appeared off Jamestown. At once the Virginians made ready to resist; cannon were mounted; the Cavaliers turned out in force, sword by side, gun in hand. Then a little boat flying a white flag was seen to put off for the shore. It was a messenger from the British captain.

It would be much better for them, he said, to yield peacefully than to fight and be beaten. For hold out against the great strength of Britain they could not. His words had weight with the Virginians. Yet long and seriously they debated. Some would have held out, but others saw only misery and destruction in such a course. So at length they surrendered to the might of Cromwell.

The conditions were not severe. They had to submit and take the oath of allegiance to the British Parliament. Those who refused were given a year's time in which to leave the colony. And as for their love of the King? Why, they might pray for him, and drink his health in private, and no man would hinder them. Only in public such things would not be tolerated.

In bitterness of heart the Cavalier Governor Berkeley gave up his post, sold his house in Jamestown, and went away to live in his great country house at Green Spring. Here amid his apple-trees and orchards he lived in a sort of rural state, riding forth in his great coach, and welcoming with open arms the Cavaliers who came to him for aid and comfort in those evil times.

These Cavaliers were men and women of good family. They came from the great houses of England, and in their new homes they continued to lead much the same life as they had done at home. So in Virginia there grew up a Cavalier society, a society of men and women accustomed to command, accustomed to be waited upon, who drove about in gilded coaches, and dressed in silks and velvets. Thus the plain Virginian farmer became a country squire. From these Cavalier families were descended George Washington, James Madison and other great men who helped to make America.

The years of the Commonwealth passed quietly in Virginia. Having made the colonists submit, the Parliament left them to themselves, and Virginia for the first time was absolutely self-governing. But the great Protector died, the Restoration followed, when the careless, pleasure-loving King Charles II was set upon the throne.

In Virginia, too, there was a little Restoration. When the news was brought, the Cavaliers flung up their caps and shouted for joy. Bonfires were lit, bells were rung and guns fired, and to the sound of drum and trumpet Charles by the Grace of God King of England, Scotland, France, Ireland and Virginia was proclaimed to all the winds of heaven. A new seal was made upon which were the words "*En dat Virginia quintum,*" meaning "Behold Virginia gives the fifth (dominion)." Henceforth Virginia was often called by the name of the "Old Dominion."

Nor was that all. For with the Restoration of the Stuarts, Berkeley, too, was restored. The haughty Cavalier left his country manor house and came back to rule at Jamestown once more, as Governor and Captain General of Virginia.

During the Commonwealth there had been little change made in the government of Virginia, except that the right of voting for the Burgesses had been given to a much larger number of people.

That did not please Sir William Berkeley at all. He took away the right from a good many people. When he came back to power, he found the House of Burgesses much to his liking. So instead of having it re-elected every year, he kept the same members for fourteen years lest the people should elect others who would not do his bidding.

This made the people discontented. But they soon had greater causes for discontent. First there was the Navigation Law. This Law had been passed ten years before, but it had never really been put in force in America. By this Law it was ordered that no goods should be exported from the colonies in America except in British ships. Further it was ordered that the colonies should not trade with any country save England and Ireland or "any of the said Lands, Islands, Plantations, or Territories" of England. It was a foolish law, meant to hurt the Dutch, and put gold into the pockets of British merchants. Instead it drove the colonies to rebellion.

Virginia had yet another grievance. Virginia, which for eight years had been self-governing, Virginia which had begun to feel that she had a life of her own, a place of her own among the nations, suddenly found herself given away like some worthless chattel to two of the King's favorites - the Earl of Arlington and Lord Culpeper.

The careless, laughter-loving King owed much to his friends who had rescued him from beggary and set him upon his father's throne. Here was an easy way of repaying two of them. If they really desired that wild land beyond the seas, where no civilized people lived, and where the weed which his pompous grandfather had disliked so much grew, why they should have it! So he carelessly signed his royal name and for a yearly rent of forty shillings all that "dominion of land and water commonly called Virginia" was theirs for the space of thirty-one years.

It was but a scratch of the pen to the King. It was everything to the Virginians, and when news of it reached them, all Virginia was ablaze. They who had clung to the King in his evil days, they who had been the last people belonging to England to submit to the Commonwealth, to be thus tossed to his favorites like some useless toy, without so much as a by your leave! They would not suffer it. And they sent a messenger to England to lay their case before the King.

As to Charles, he was lazily astonished to find that anyone objected to such a little trifle. And with his usual idle good nature, he promised that it should be altered. But he had no intention of hurrying. Meanwhile out in Virginia, events were hastening.

Notes:

"I thank God there are no free schools" can be found in The Statutes at Large: Being a Collection of all the Laws of Virginia, *Volume II.*

The quote about "depart the colony" was from the March session of the General Assembly, 1642-3, 2nd Revisal of the Laws of Virginia and the 64 Act: "And that the Gov: and Counsel do take care that all nonconformists, upon notice of them, shall be compelled to depart the colony with all convenience." The Virginia Magazine of History and Biography, Vol. 5, No. 1 *(Jul., 1897), p. 108.*

"In horror and despairs" can be found in William and Mary College Quarterly Historical Magazine, *published by College of William and Mary in 1910, Volume 18, p. 118.*

The quotes from the October 1649 meeting of the House of Burgesses are from William Berkeley's proclamation about the beheading of Charles I, and they can be read in Americana: (American Historical Magazine), *Volume 4, p.9 (published 1909).*

The Navigation Acts were a series of laws beginning in the 1650's. They would eventually be repealed in 1849.

Chapter 20

Bacon's Rebellion

For some time now there were increasing conflicts between different Native tribes and the Virginia settlers, especially along the frontier. Many Indians, some already displaced from other areas, had grown restless and uneasy at the constantly widening borders of the settlements. Day by day the forest was cleared, the cornfields stretched farther and farther inland, and these first inhabitants saw themselves driven farther and farther from their hunting-ground.

Some tribes and settlers continued to engage in trade with one another. One particular dispute over payment grew into retribution, then an attack, then a counterattack, which led to retaliation and bloodshed. There was a reprisal that targeted the wrong tribe, and the ensuing fighting threatened to escalate into war. The Virginian farmers along the James River feared for their farms, as day by day the tale of horror grew, till it seemed at length that no farm along the borders of the colony was safe from destruction. Yet Governor Berkeley did nothing.

The Virginians felt helpless against his slow response. This longtime governor was now a traitor to their trust, they declared, and feared to wage war on the Indians lest it should spoil his fur trade with them. But that was not so. A deadlier fear than that kept Berkeley idle. He knew how his tyranny had made the people hate him, and he feared to arm them and lead them against the tribes, lest having subdued these foes they should turn their arms against him.

161

But the farmers of Virginia, also battling a poor tobacco crop from the last year's drought, were seething with discontent and ripe for rebellion. All they wanted was a leader, and soon they found one. This leader was Nathaniel Bacon, a wealthy young Englishman who had but lately come to the colony. He was dashing and handsome, had winning ways and a persuasive tongue. He was the very man for a popular leader, and soon at his back he had an army of three hundred armed settlers, "one and all at his devotion."

Bacon then sent to the Governor asking for a commission to go against the Indians. But Berkeley put him off with one excuse after another; until at length goaded into rebellion, Bacon and his men determined to set out, commission or no commission.

But they had not gone far when a messenger came spurring behind them in hot haste. He came with a proclamation from the Governor denouncing them all as rebels and bidding them disperse at once on pain of forfeiting their lands and goods. Some obeyed, but the rest went on with Bacon, and only returned after having routed the Indians. Their defeat was so severe that the battle is known as the Battle of Bloody Run, because it was said the blood of the Indians made red the stream which flowed near the battlefield.

The Indians for the time were cowed, and Bacon marched slowly home with his men.

Meanwhile Berkeley had gathered horses and men and had ridden out to crush this turbulent youth. But hearing suddenly that the people had risen in revolt, he hastened back to Jamestown with all speed. He saw he must do something to appease the people. So he dissolved the House of Burgesses, which for fourteen years had done his bidding, and ordered a new election. This pacified the people somewhat. But they actually elected the rebel Bacon as one of the members of the House.

Bacon was not, however, altogether to escape the consequences of his bold deeds. As soon as he returned he was taken prisoner and led before the Governor. The stern old Cavalier received this rebel with cool civility.

"Mr. Bacon," he said, "have you forgot to be a gentleman?"

"No, may it please your honor," answered Bacon.

"Then," said the Governor, "I will take your parole."

So Bacon was set free until the House of Burgesses should meet. Meantime he was given to understand that if he made open confession of his misdeeds in having marched against the Indians without a commission, he would be forgiven, receive his commission, and be allowed to fight again. It was not easy to make this proud young man bend his knee. But to gain his end Bacon consented to beg forgiveness for what he deemed no offence. The Governor meant it to be a solemn occasion, one not lightly to be forgotten. So when the burgesses and council were gathered the Governor stood up.

"If there be joy in the presence of the angels over one sinner that repenteth," he said, "there is joy now, for we have a penitent sinner come before us. Call Mr. Bacon."

The doors were thrown wide open and in marched Bacon, tall and proud, looking grave indeed but little like a repentant sinner. At the bar of the House, he knelt on one knee, and reading from a paper written out for him confessed his crimes, begging pardon from God, the King, and the Governor.

When his clear young voice ceased, the old Governor spoke.

"God forgive you," he said, solemnly. "I forgive you." Three times he repeated the words and was silent.

"And all that were with him?" asked one of the council.

"Yea," said the Governor, "and all that were with him."

Thus the matter seemed ended. There was peace again and the House could now proceed to further business.

Part of that business was to settle what was to be done about the Indian war. Some of the people hoped that they might get help from Native people who had been friendly to them. So the Queen of the Pamunkeys, Cockacoeske, had been asked to come to the Assembly and say what help she would give. Her tribe was part of that same confederacy over which the Powhatan had ruled so long ago. And although it was now but a shadow of its former self, she had still about a hundred and fifty braves at command whose help the Englishmen were anxious to gain.

Queen Cockacoeske entered the Assembly with great dignity, and with an air of majesty walked slowly up the long room. Her walk was so graceful, her gestures so courtly, that everyone looked at her in admiration. Upon her head she wore a crown of black and white wampum. Her robe was made of deerskin and covered her from shoulders to feet, the edges of it being slit into fringes six inches deep. At her right hand walked an English interpreter, at her left her son, John West, a youth of twenty.

When Queen Cockacoeske reached the table she stood still, looking at the members coldly and gravely, and only at their urgent request did she sit down. Beside her, as they had entered the room, stood her son and interpreter on either hand.

When she was seated the chairman asked her how many men she would send to help them against their enemy. All those present were quite sure that she understood English, but she would not speak to the chairman direct, and answered him through her interpreter, bidding him speak to her son.

The young Pamunkey chieftain however, also refused to reply. So again the Queen was urged to say how many men she could send.

For some minutes she sat still, as if in deep thought. Then in a shrill high voice full of passionate fervor, and trembling as if with tears, she spoke in her own tongue, and ever and anon amid the tragic torrent of sound, the words "Totopotomoi chepiack, Totopotomoi chepiack" could be heard.

Few present understood her. But one of the members did and shook his head sadly.

"What she says is too true, to our shame be it said," he sighed. "My father was general in that battle of which she speaks. Totopotomoi was her husband, and he led a hundred men against our enemies, and was there slain with most of his company. And from that day to this no recompense has been given to her. Therefore she upbraids us, and cries, 'Totopotomoi is dead.'"

When they heard the reason for the Queen's anger, many were filled with sympathy for her.

The chairman, however, was a crusty old fellow, and he was quite unmoved by the poor Queen's passion of grief and anger. Never a word did he say to comfort her distress, not a sign of sympathy did he give. He rudely brushed aside her vehement appeal and repeated his question.

"What men will you give to help against the enemy Indians?"

With quivering nostrils, and flashing eyes, Queen Cockacoeske drew herself up scornfully, looked at him, then turned her face away, and sat mute.

Three times he repeated his question.

Then in a low disdainful voice, her head still turned away, she muttered in her own language "Six."

This would never do. The lumbering old chairman argued and persuaded, while the majestic Queen sat sullenly silent. At length she uttered one word as scornfully as the last. "Twelve," she said. Then rising, she walked proudly and gravely from the hall.

Thus did the blundering old fellow of a chairman, for the lack of a few kindly words, turn away the hearts of an allied tribe, and lose their help at a moment when it was sorely needed.

The new House had many other things to discuss besides these wars, and the people, who had been kept out of their rights for so long, now made up for lost time. They passed laws with feverish haste. They restored manhood suffrage, did away with many class privileges, and in various ways instituted reforms. Afterwards these laws were known as Bacon's Laws.

But meanwhile Bacon was preparing a new surprise for everyone.

One morning the town was agog with news. "Bacon has fled, Bacon has fled!" cried everyone.

It was true. Bacon had grown tired of waiting for the commission which never came. So he was off to raise the country. A few days later he marched back again at the head of six hundred men.

At two o'clock one bright June day, the sounds of drum and trumpet were heard mingled with the tramp of feet and the clatter of horses' hoofs. And General Bacon, as folk began to call him now, drew up his men not an arrow's flight from the State House.

The people of Jamestown rushed to the spot. Every window and balcony was crowded with eager excited people. Men, women and children jostled each other on the green, as Bacon, with a file of soldiers on either hand, marched to the State House.

The white-haired old Governor, shaking with anger, came out to meet the insolent young rebel. With trembling fingers he tore at the fine lace ruffles of his shirt, baring his breast.

"Here I am!" he cried. "Shoot me! 'Fore God 'tis a fair mark. Shoot me! Shoot me!" he repeated in a frenzy.

But Bacon answered peaceably enough. "No, may it please your honor," he said, "we will not hurt a hair of your head, nor of any other man's. We are come for a commission to save our lives from the Indians which you have so often promised. And now we will have it before we go."

But when the stern old Cavalier refused to listen to him, Bacon, too, lost his temper, and laying his hand on his sword, swore he would kill the Governor, Council, Assembly and all, rather than forego his commission. His men, too, grew impatient and filled the air with their shouts.

"We will have it, we will have it!" they cried, at the same time pointing their loaded guns at the windows of the State House.

Minute by minute the uproar increased, till at length one of the Burgesses, going to a window, waved his handkerchief ("a pacifeck handkercher" a quaint old record calls it) and shouted, "You shall have it, you shall have it."

So the tumult was quieted. A commission was drawn up making Bacon Commander-in-Chief of the army against the Indians, and a letter was written to the King praising him for what he had done against them. But the stern old Governor was still unbending, and not till next day was he browbeaten into signing both papers.

The young rebel had triumphed. But Berkeley was not yet done with him, for the same ship which carried the letter of the Burgesses to the King also carried a private letter from Berkeley in which he gave his own account of the business. "I have for above thirty years governed the most flourishing country the sun ever shone over," he wrote, "but am now encompassed with rebellion like waters."

And as soon as Bacon was safely away, and at grips once more with the Indians, the Governor again proclaimed him and his followers to be rebels and traitors.

Bacon had well-nigh crushed the foe when this news was brought to him, yet he was cut to the quick by the injustice.

"I am vexed to the heart," he said, "for to think that while I am hunting Indian wolves, tigers, and foxes which daily destroy our harmless sheep and lambs, that I, and those with me, should be pursued with a full cry, as a more savage and no less ravenous beast."

So now in a dangerous mood he marched back to Jamestown. Things were looking dark for him, but his men were with him heart and soul. When one of them, a Scotsman named Drummond, was warned that this was rebellion, he replied recklessly, "I am in over shoes, I will be in over boots."

His wife was even more bold. "This is dangerous work," said someone, "and England will have something to say to it." Then Sarah Drummond picked up a twig, and snapping it in two, threw it down again. "I fear the power of England no more than that broken straw," she cried.

Bacon now issued a manifesto in reply to Berkeley's proclamation, declaring that he and his followers could not find in their hearts one single spot of rebellion or treason. "Let Truth be bold," he cried, "and let all the world know the real facts of this matter." He appealed to the King against Sir William, who had levied unjust taxes, who had failed to protect the people against the Native people, who had traded unjustly with them, and done much evil to his Majesty's true subjects.

So far there had only been bitter words between the old Governor and the young rebel, and Bacon had never drawn his sword save against the Indians. Now he turned it against the Governor, and, marching on Jamestown, burned it to the ground, and Berkeley, defeated, fled to Accomac on the Eastern Shore.

Everywhere Bacon seemed successful, and from Jamestown he marched northward to settle affairs there also "after his own measures." But a grim and all-conquering captain had now taken up arms against this victorious rebel, Captain Death, whom even the greatest soldier must obey. And on October 1, 1676, Bacon laid down his sword forever. He had been the heart and soul of the rebellion, and with his death it collapsed swiftly and completely.

Bacon was now beyond the Governor's wrath, but he wreaked his vengeance on those who had followed him. For long months the rebels were hunted and hounded, and when caught they were hanged without mercy. The first to suffer was Colonel Thomas Hansford. He was a brave man and a gentleman, and all he asked was that he might be shot like a soldier, and not hanged like a dog. But the wrathful Governor would not listen to his appeal, and he was hanged. On the scaffold he spoke to those around, praying them to remember that he died a loyal subject of the King and a lover of his country. He has been called the first martyr to American liberty.

Another young Major named Cheesman was condemned to death, but died in prison, some say by poison.

The Governor, when Cheesman was brought before him, asked fiercely: "What reason had you for rebellion?"

But before the Major could reply, his young wife stepped from the surrounding crowd and threw herself upon her knees before the Governor. "It was my doing," she cried. "I persuaded him, and but for me he would never have done it. I am guilty, not he. I pray you therefore let me be hanged, and he be pardoned."

But the old Cavalier's heart was filled to overflowing with a frenzy of hate. He was utterly untouched by the poor lady's brave and sad appeal, and answered her only with bitter, insulting words.

Drummond, too, was taken. He was indeed "in over boots" and fearless to the last. The Governor was overjoyed at his capture, and with mocking ceremony swept his hat from his head, and, bowing low, cried exultantly, "Mr. Drummond, you are very welcome. I am more glad to see you than any man in Virginia. Mr. Drummond, you shall be hanged in half an hour."

"What your honor pleases," calmly replied Drummond. And so he died.

It seemed as if the Governor's vengeance would never be satisfied. But at length the House met, and petitioned him to spill no more blood. "For," said one of the members, "had we let him alone he would have hanged half the country."

News of his wild doings, too, were carried home, and reached even the King's ears. "That old fool," cried he, "has slain more men in that naked country than I did for the murder of my father." So Berkeley was recalled.

At his going the whole colony rejoiced. Guns were fired and bonfires lit to celebrate the passing of the tyrant.

Berkeley did not live long after his downfall. He had hoped that when he saw the King, and explained to him his cause, that he would be again received into favor. But his hopes were vain. The King refused to see him, and he who had given up everything, even good name and fame, in his King's cause, died broken-hearted a few months later.

Notes:

Nathaniel Bacon was Governor Berkeley's cousin by marriage. (Lady Berkeley, Frances Culpeper, was Bacon's cousin.)

"One and all at his devotion" comes from the account of Robert Beverley on Bacon's Rebellion, written in 1704.

The Pamunkey tribe is the first of eleven Virginia tribes to receive federal recognition. "The United States Department of the Interior announced final determination to acknowledge the Pamunkey Indian Tribe (Petitioner #323) as a federally recognized Indian tribe on July 2, 2015 with the effective decision date of January 28, 2016." From the Pamunkey. org website.

Wampum refers to strings of polished shells. Wearing wampum indicated a person's authority. It was also used in religious ceremonies, or as a way to secure peace between tribes.

Some of the quotes in this chapter can be found in **William and Mary Quarterly,** *Historical Magazine, Volume XVIII, 1910.*

Suffrage means the right to vote.

Nathaniel Bacon was at first seen as a rebel, but then later as a patriot, based on Thomas Jefferson's gathering of Virginia's records and papers. "Jefferson made his own exact transcription of Mathew's account of Bacon's Rebellion and arranged for its publication in 'The Enquirer' (Richmond, Virginia). Jefferson's transcription was published in installments in **The Enquirer**, *September 1, 5, and 8, 1804." (Thomas Jefferson's papers, Virginia records 1606-1737, Library of Congress) (Thomas Mathew was a contemporary observer of Bacon's Rebellion, and he wrote his account in 1705.) In recent years, however, Bacon's Rebellion has been seen more as a struggle between two leaders.*

Pronunciation Guide:

Cockacoeske – coke-uh-COW-ski

Totopotomoi – tot-uh-POT-uh-mee

Chapter 21

The Story of the Knights of the Golden Horseshoe

Bacon was driven into rebellion by evil government and tyranny. But the rising did little good. Bacon's Laws were done away with and Lord Culpeper, one of the two nobles to whom Charles II had given Virginia, came out as Governor. He soon showed himself a greedy tyrant, caring nothing for the happiness of his people, and bent only on making money for himself.

Other governors followed him, many of them worthless, some never taking the trouble to come to Virginia at all. They stayed at home, accepting large sums of money, and letting other people do the work. But they were not all worthless and careless. Some were good, and one of the best was a Scotsman, Alexander Spotswood. He was a lieutenant governor. That is, the Governor in name was the Earl of Orkney, who was given the post as a reward for his great services as a soldier. But he never crossed the Atlantic to visit his noble province. Instead he sent others to rule for him. They were in fact the real governors, although they were called lieutenant governors.

Spotswood loved Virginia, and he did all he could to make the colony prosperous. He saw that the land was rich in minerals, and that much could be done with iron ore. So he built smelting furnaces, and altogether was so eager over it that he was called the Tubal-Cain of Virginia. For Tubal-Cain, you remember, "was an instructor of every artificer in brass and iron."

Spotswood also planted vines and brought over a colony of Germans to teach the people how to grow them properly and make wine. It was he, too, who first explored what they called the West.

Virginia up till now had lain between the sea and the blue range of mountains which cut it off from the land behind. To the English, that was a land utterly unknown. All they knew was that the French were claiming it. But Governor Spotswood wanted to know more. So one August he gathered a company of friends and set forth on an exploring expedition. With servants and four guides from the Meherrin tribe they made a party of about fifty or so, and a jolly company they were. They hunted by the way and camped beneath the stars. There was no lack of food and drink, and it was more like a prolonged picnic than an exploring expedition.

The explorers reached the Blue Ridge, and, climbing to the top of a pass, looked down upon the beautiful wild valley beyond, through which wound a shining river. Spotswood called the river the Euphrates. But fortunately the name did not stick, and it is still called by its beautiful Native name of Shenandoah.

Spotswood named the highest peak he saw Mount George in honor of the King, and his companions gave the next highest peak the name of Mount Alexander in honor of the Governor whose Christian name was Alexander. Then they went down into the valley below, and on the banks of the river they buried a bottle, inside which they had put a paper declaring that the whole valley belonged to George I, King by the Grace of God of Great Britain, France, Ireland, and Virginia.

After that the merry party turned homewards. They climbed to the top of the gap, took a last look at the fair valley of the unknown West, and then went down once more into the familiar plains of Virginia.

For this expedition all the horses were shod with iron, a thing very unusual in Virginia where there were no hard or stony roads. So as a remembrance of their pleasant time together, Spotswood gave each of his companions a miniature gold horseshoe set with precious stones for nails. Graven upon them were the Latin words, *Sic juvat transcendere montes* which mean, "Thus it is a pleasure to cross the mountains."

Later all those who took part in the expedition were called Knights of the Golden Horseshoe.

Up to about this time the people in Virginia had been altogether English. Now a change came.

In France, Louis XIV was persecuting the Protestants, or Huguenots, as they were called. He ordered them all to become Catholics or die, and he forbade them to leave the country. But thousands of them refused to give up their religion, and in spite of the King's commands they stole away from the country by secret ways. Many of them found a refuge in America.

In the north of Ireland, which had been settled chiefly by Scotsmen, the Presbyterians were being persecuted by the Church of England; at the same time the English Parliament was hampering their trade with unfair laws. So to escape from this double persecution, many Scotch-Irish fled to America.

In Germany, too, the Protestants were being persecuted by the Catholic Princes. They, too, fled to America.

All these widely varying refugees found new homes in other colonies as well as in Virginia, as we shall presently hear. In Virginia, it was chiefly to the Shenandoah Valley that they came, that valley which Spotswood and his knights of the Golden Horseshoe had seen and claimed for King George. The coming of these new people changed Virginia a good deal.

After the death of King Charles, the coming of the Cavaliers had made Virginia Royalist and aristocratic, so now the coming of those persecuted Protestants and Presbyterians tended to make it democratic. That is, the coming of the Cavaliers increased the number of those who believed in the government of the many by the few. The coming of the European Protestants increased the number of those who believed in the government of the people by the people.

So in the House of Burgesses, there were scenes of excitement. But these were no longer in Jamestown, for the capital had been removed to Williamsburg. Jamestown, you remember, had been burned by Bacon. Lord Culpeper, however, rebuilt it. But a few years later it was again burned down by accident. It had never been a healthy spot; no one seemed very anxious to build it again, so it was forsaken, and Williamsburg became and remained the capital for nearly a hundred years.

Today all that is left of Jamestown, the first home of Englishmen in America, is the ivy-grown ruin of the church.

Notes:

Scripture about Tubal-Cain taken from Genesis 4:22.

Regarding the expedition to the west: "On the twenty-sixth of August Spotswood was joined here by several gentlemen, two small companies of rangers, and four Meherrin Indians," from Alexander Spotswood's Transmontane Expedition, from History of the Colony and Ancient Dominion of Virginia, *by Charles Campbell (Philadelphia: J. B. Lippincott and Co., 1860), p.387.*

The tribe now goes by Kauwets'a:ka, their original name.

Jamestown Settlement is now a living-history museum a little over a mile from the original site of the colony. It was first created for the 350th anniversary of Jamestown in 1957.

While governor, Alexander Spotswood was also involved in bringing the right of habeas corpus (the requirement for a government to show a legal reason to detain someone) to the colony, in sending warships to capture Blackbeard the pirate (Edward Teach), and in forming a treaty with the Nottoway (Cheroenhaka) tribe. The Spotswood Treaty Tribute of three peace arrows wrapped in a beaver pelt and wampum belt continues annually to this very day.

Pronunciation Guide:

Meherrin – mee-HAIR-in

Chapter 22

The Story of the Pilgrim Fathers

While the Colony of Virginia was fighting for life and struggling against tyranny, other colonies were taking root upon the wide shores of America.

You will remember that in 1606, a sort of double company of adventurers was formed in England, one branch of which - the London Company - founded Jamestown. The other branch - the Plymouth Company - also sent out an expedition and tried to found a colony at the mouth of the Kennebec River in what is now Maine. But it was a failure. Some of the adventurers were so discouraged with the cold and bleak appearance of the land that they sailed home again in the ship which had brought them out. Only about forty-five or so stayed on. The winter was long and cold, and they were so weary of it, so homesick and miserable, that when in the spring a ship came out with provisions, they all left Popham Colony and sailed home again. Remarkably, only one of their original number had died. However, they had nothing good to say of Virginia, as the whole land was then called by the English. It was far too cold, and no place for Englishmen, they said.

Still some of the adventurers of the Plymouth Company did not give up hope of founding a colony. And nine years after this first attempt, our old friend Captain John Smith, recovered from his wounds received in Virginia and as vigorous as ever, sailed out to North Virginia. In the first place he went "to take whales, and also to make trials of a mine of gold and of copper" and in the long run he hoped to found a colony.

It was he who changed the name from North Virginia to New England, by which name it has ever since been known. He also named the great river which he found there Charles River after Prince Charles, who later became King Charles I, and all along the coast he marked places with the names of English towns, one of which he named Plymouth.

But Smith did not succeed in founding a colony in New England, and several adventurers who followed him had no better success. The difficulties to be overcome were great, and in order to found a colony on that inhospitable coast, men of tremendous purpose and endurance were needed. At length, these men appeared.

Nowadays a man may believe what he likes either in the way of politics or religion. He may belong to any political party he pleases, or he may belong to none. He may write and make speeches about his opinions. Probably no one will listen to him; certainly, he will not be imprisoned for mere opinions. It is the same with religion. A man may go to any church he likes or go to none. He may write books or preach sermons, and no one will hinder him.

But in the days of King James, things were very different. In those days there was little freedom either in thought or action, in religion or politics. As we have seen, King James could not endure the thought that his colony should be self-governing and free to make laws for itself. Consequently, he took its charter away. In religion it was just the same. In England at the Reformation, the King had been made head of the Church. And if people did not believe what the King and Clergy told them to believe, they were sure, sooner or later, to be punished for it.

Now in England more and more people began to think for themselves on matters of religion. More and more people found it difficult to believe as King and Clergy wished them to believe. Some found the Church of England far too like the old Church of Rome. They wanted to do away with all pomp and ceremony and have things quite simple. They did not wish to separate from the Church; they only wanted to make the Church clean and pure of all its errors. So they got the name of Puritans. Others, however, quite despaired of making the Church pure. They desired to leave it altogether and set up a Church of their own. They were called Separatists, or sometimes, from the name of a man who was one of their chief leaders, Brownists.

These Brownists did not want to have bishops and priests, and they would not own the King as head of the Church. Instead of going to church they used to meet together in private houses, there to pray to God in the manner in which their own hearts told them was right. This, of course, was considered treason and foul wickedness. So on all hands the Brownists were persecuted. They were fined and imprisoned, some were even hanged. But all this persecution was in vain, and the number of Separatists instead of decreasing increased as years went on.

Now at Scrooby, a tiny village in Nottinghamshire, England, and in other villages round, both in Nottinghamshire and Lincolnshire, there were a number of Separatists. Every Sunday these people would walk long distances to some appointed place, very likely to Scrooby, or to Babworth, where there was a grave and reverent preacher, to hold their meetings.

But they were never left long in peace. They were hunted and persecuted on every side, till at length they decided to go to Holland where they heard there was freedom of religion for all men.

To many of them, this was a desperate adventure. In those days, few men traveled. For the most part people lived and died without once leaving their native villages. To go into a new country, to learn a new language, to get their living they know not how, seemed to some a misery almost worse than death. Still they determined to go, such was their eagerness to serve God aright.

The going was not easy. They were harassed and hindered in every fashion. Again and again, evil men cheated them and robbed them of almost all they possessed, leaving them starving and penniless upon the seashore. But at length, overcoming all difficulties, in one way or another, they all reached Amsterdam.

Even here, however, they did not find the full freedom and peace which they desired, and they next moved to Leyden.

They found it "a fair and beautiful city and of a sweet situation." Here they settled down and for some years lived in comfort, earning their living by weaving and such employments, and worshipping God at peace in their own fashion.

But after about eleven or twelve years, they began once more to think of moving. They had many reasons for this, one being that if they stayed longer in Holland their children and grandchildren would forget how to speak English, and in a few generations they would no longer be English, but Dutch. So they determined to go to some place where they could still remain English, and yet worship God as they thought right.

And the place their thoughts turned to was the vast country of America. But which part of America they could not at first decide. After much talk, however, they at length decided to ask the Virginian Company to allow them to settle in their land, but as a separate colony, so that they might still have religious freedom.

Two messengers were therefore dispatched to London to arrange matters with the company. The Virginian Company was quite willing to have these Separatists as settlers. But do what they would, they could not get the King to promise them freedom to worship God. All that they could wring from him was a promise that he would take no notice of them so long as they behaved peaceably. To allow or tolerate them by his public authority, under his broad seal, was not to be thought of.

That was the best the Virginian Company or any of their friends could do for the Separatists. And with this answer the messengers were obliged to return to Leyden. When the English men and women there heard it, they were much disturbed. Some felt that without better assurance of peace they would be foolish to leave their safe refuge. But the greater part decided that poor though the assurance was they would be well to go, trusting in God to bring them safely out of all their troubles. And after all they reflected "a seal as broad as the house floor would not serve the turn" if James did not wish to keep his promise, so little trust did they put in princes and their oaths.

So it was decided to go to the New World, and after much trouble everything was got ready. A little ship called the *Speedwell* was bought and fitted up. Then those who had determined to go went down to the seashore, accompanied by all their friends.

Their hearts were heavy as they left the beautiful city which had been their home for the last twelve years. But they knew that they were pilgrims and strangers upon the earth, and they looked only to find in heaven an abiding place. So steadfastly they set their faces towards the sea. They went on board, their friends following sorrowfully. Then came the sad parting. They clung to each other with tears, their words of farewell and prayers broken by sobs. It was so pitiful a sight that even among the Dutchmen who looked on there was scarce a dry eye.

At length, the time came when the last farewell had to be said. Then Pastor Robinson fell upon his knees on the deck, and as they knelt round him, he lifted his hands to heaven, and with tears running down his cheeks prayed God to bless them all.

So the sails were hoisted and the *Speedwell* sailed away to Southampton. Here she found the *Mayflower* awaiting her, and the two set forth together. But they had not gone far before the captain of the *Speedwell* complained that his ship was leaking so badly that he dared not go on. So both ships put in to Dartmouth, and here the *Speedwell* was thoroughly overhauled and mended, and again they set out.

But still the captain declared that the *Speedwell* was leaking. So once more the pilgrims put back, this time to Plymouth. And here it was decided that the *Speedwell* was unseaworthy, and unfit to venture across the great ocean. That she was a rotten little boat is fairly certain, but it is also fairly certain that the Captain did not want to sail to America, and therefore he made the worst, instead of the best, of his ship.

If it is true that he did not want to cross the ocean, he now had his way. For the *Speedwell* was sent back to London with all those who had already grown tired of the venture, or who had grown fearful because of the many mishaps. And the *Mayflower,* taking the rest of the passengers from the *Speedwell* and as many of the stores as she could find room for, proceeded upon her voyage alone.

Among those who sailed in her were Captain Miles Standish and Master Mullins, with his fair young daughter Priscilla. I daresay you have read the story Longfellow made about them and John Alden. At the first, John Alden did not go as a Pilgrim. He was hired at Southampton as a cooper, merely for the voyage, and was free to go home again if he wished. But he stayed, and as we know from Longfellow's poem, he married Priscilla.

Now at length these Pilgrim Fathers, as we have learned to call them, were really on their way. But all the trouble about the *Speedwell* had meant a terrible loss of time, and although the Pilgrims bad left Holland in July, it was September before they finally set sail from Plymouth, and their voyage was really begun.

And now instead of having fair they had foul weather. For days and nights, with every sail reefed, they were driven hither and thither by the wind, were battered and beaten by cruel waves, and tossed helplessly from side to side. At length after two months of terror and hardships, they sighted the shores of America.

They had, however, been driven far out of their course, and instead of being near the mouth of the Hudson River and within the area granted to the Virginian Company, they were much further north, near Cape Cod, and within the area granted to the Plymouth Company, where they had really no legal right to land. So although they were joyful indeed to see land, they decided to sail southward to the mouth of the Hudson, more especially as the weather was now better.

Soon, however, as they sailed south, they found themselves among dangerous shoals and roaring breakers, and, being in terror of shipwreck, they turned back again. And when they once more reached the shelter of Cape Cod harbor, they fell on their knees and most heartily thanked God, Who had brought them safely over the furious ocean and delivered them from all its perils and miseries.

They vowed no more to risk the fury of the tempest, but to settle where they were in the hope of being able to make things right with the Plymouth Company later on. So in the little cabin of the *Mayflower* the Pilgrims held a meeting, at which they chose a Governor and drew up a Compact which began "In the name of God, Amen." They all promised to obey these rules for the government of the colony. But this done they found it difficult to decide just what would be the best place for their little town, and they spent a month or more exploring the coast round about. At length they settled upon a spot.

On Captain John Smith's map, it was already marked Plymouth, and so the Pilgrims decided to call the town Plymouth because of this, and also because Plymouth was the last town in England at which they had touched. So here they all went ashore, choosing as a landing place a flat rock which may be seen to this day, and which is now known as the Plymouth Rock.

"Which had been to their feet as a doorstep,
Into a world unknown—the corner-stone of a nation!"

The Pilgrim Fathers had now safely passed the perils of the sea. But many more troubles and miseries were in store for them. For hundreds of miles the country lay barren and untilled, inhabited by Native people, the nearest British settlement being five hundred miles away. There was no one upon the shore to greet them, no friendly lights, no smoke arising from cheerful cottage fires, no sign of outward habitation far or near. It was a silent, frost-bound coast upon which they had set foot.

The weather was bitterly cold and the frost so keen that even their clothes were frozen stiff. And ere these Pilgrims could find a shelter from the winter blasts, trees had to be felled and hewn for the building of their houses. It was enough to make the stoutest heart quake. Yet not one among this little band of Pilgrims flinched or thought of turning back. They were made of sterner stuff than that, and they put all their trust in God.

"May not and ought not the children of those fathers rightly say," writes William Bradford, who was their Governor for thirty-one years, "our fathers were Englishmen which came over this great ocean and were ready to perish in the wilderness? But they cried unto the Lord and He heard their voice and looked on their adversity."

The winter was an unusually severe one. And so, having no homes to shelter them or comfort of any kind, many of the Pilgrims died. Many more became seriously ill. Indeed, at one time there were not more than six or seven out of a hundred and more who were well and able to work. And had it not been for the wonderful devotion and loving kindness of these few, the whole colony might have perished miserably. But these few worked with a will, felling trees, cooking meals, caring for the sick both day and night.

The first winter the Pilgrim Fathers, Bradford said, was difficult, though "they had borne their sad afflictions with as much patience and contentedness as I think any people could do." But at length spring came, and with the coming of warmth and sunshine the sickness disappeared. The sun seemed to put new life into everyone. So when in April the Mayflower, which had been in harbor all winter, sailed homeward, not one of the Pilgrims sailed with her.

The little white-winged ship was the last link with home. They had but to step on board to be wafted back to the green hedgerows and meadows bright with daisies and buttercups in dear old England. It was a terrible temptation. Yet not one yielded to it. With tears streaming down their faces, the Pilgrims knelt upon the shore and saw the Mayflower go, following her with prayers and blessings until she was out of sight. Then they went back to their daily labors. Only when they looked out to sea, the harbor seemed very empty with no friendly little vessel lying there.

Meanwhile among all the miseries of the winter, there had been one bright spot. The Pilgrims had made friends with the Native people. They had often noticed them with fear "skulking about those who were ashore." Once when they had left tools lying about, they had been stolen. But whenever they tried to get speech with the Native people, they fled away.

What was their surprise then when one morning "a certain Indian came boldly among them" and spoke to them in broken English!

He told them that his name was Samoset, and that he was the Englishmen's friend. He also said he could tell them of another Indian called Squanto who could speak better English than he could. This Squanto had been stolen away from his Patuxet tribe by a wicked captain who intended to sell him as a slave to Spain. But he had escaped to England, and later by the help of Englishmen, he had been brought back to his home. All his tribe, however, had meantime been swept away by a plague, and now only he remained.

Samoset also said that his great sachem named Massasoit wished to make friends with the Englishmen. The settlers were well pleased to find Samoset ready to be friendly and, giving him presents of a few beads and bits of colored cloth, they sent him away happy. But very soon he returned, bringing Squanto and Massasoit with him. Then there was a very solemn meeting; the Native men, gorgeous in paint and feathers, sat beside the sad-faced Englishmen in their tall black hats and sober clothes, and together they swore friendship and peace. And so long as Massasoit lived, this peace lasted.

They had a harvest that year, with "many of the Indians coming amongst us, and amongst the rest their greatest king Massasoit, with some ninety men, whom for three days we entertained and feasted, and they went out and killed five Deer, which they brought to the Plantation and bestowed on our Governor, and upon the Captain and others."

Throughout that time, Squanto stayed with the Englishmen. He taught them how to plant corn, he showed them where to fish and hunt, he was their guide through the pathless forests. He was their staunch and faithful friend, and he never left them till he died. Even then he feared to be parted from his new friends, and he begged them to "pray for him, that he might go to the Englishmen's heaven."

Besides Massasoit and the Wampanoag people, there was the Narragansett tribe, who lived to the east of the settlement, and they were by no means so friendly. At harvest time, they used to steal the corn from the fields and otherwise harass the workers. As they went unpunished, they grew ever bolder until at length one day the chief of the Narragansetts, Canonicus, sent a messenger to the Governor with a bundle of arrows tied about with a large snakeskin. This was meant as a challenge. But the Governor was not to be frightened by such threats. He sent back the snakeskin stuffed with bullets and gunpowder, and with it a bold message.

"If you would rather have war than peace," he said, "you can begin when you like. But we have done you no wrong and we do not fear you."

When the chief heard the message and saw the gunpowder and bullets, he was far too much afraid to go to war. He was too frightened to touch the snakeskin or even allow it to remain in his country but sent it back again at once.

This warlike message, however, made the settlers more careful, and they built a strong fence around their little town, with gates in it, which were shut and guarded at night. Thus the Pilgrims had peace with the Narragansetts.

They had also set matters right with the Plymouth Company and had received from them a patent or charter allowing them to settle in New England. Other Pilgrims came out from home from time to time, and the little colony prospered and grew, though slowly.

They were a grave and stern little company, obeying their Governor, fearing God, keeping the Sabbath, and regarding all other feast days as Roman Catholic, and therefore to be denounced.

It is told how one Christmas Day, the Governor called everyone out to work as usual. But some of the newcomers to the colony objected that it was against their conscience to work on Christmas Day.

The Governor looked gravely at them. "If you make it a matter of conscience," he said, "I will release you from work upon this day until you are better taught upon the matter." Then he led the others away to fell trees and saw wood. But when at noon he returned he found those, whose tender consciences had not allowed them to work, playing at ball and other games in the streets. So he went to them, and took away their balls and other toys. "For," said he, "it is against my conscience that you should play while others work."

And such was the power of the Governor that he was quietly obeyed, and we are told, "since then nothing has been attempted that way, at least openly."

They were stern, these old settlers, and perhaps to our way of thinking narrow, and they denied themselves much that is lovely in life and quite innocent. Yet we must look back at them with admiration. No people ever left their homes to go into exile for nobler ends, no colony was ever founded in a braver fashion. And it is with some regret we remember that these brave Pilgrim Fathers have given a name to no state in the great union. For the Colony of Plymouth, having held on its simple, severe way for many years, was at length swallowed up by one of its great neighbors, and became part of the State of Massachusetts. But that was not till 1692. Meanwhile, because it was the first of the New England colonies to be founded, it was often called the Old Colony.

Notes:

Quote about whales is taken from Captain John Smith's **Generall Historie,** *about his 1614 trip to New England.*

The rules drawn up on the ship are called "The Mayflower Compact," and this short document reads as follows:

"In the name of God, Amen. We whose names are under-written, the loyal subjects of our dread sovereign Lord, King James, by the grace of God, of Great Britain, France, and Ireland King, Defender of the Faith, etc.

"Having undertaken, for the glory of God, and advancement of the Christian faith, and honor of our King and Country, a voyage to plant the first colony in the northern parts of Virginia, do by these presents solemnly and mutually, in the presence of God, and one of another, covenant and combine our selves together into a civil body politic, for our better ordering and preservation and furtherance of the ends aforesaid; and by virtue hereof to enact, constitute, and frame such just and equal laws, ordinances, acts, constitutions and offices, from time to time, as shall be thought most meet and convenient for the general good of the Colony, unto which we promise all due submission and obedience. In witness whereof we have hereunder subscribed our names at Cape Cod, the

eleventh of November [New Style, November 21], in the year of the reign of our sovereign lord, King James, of England, France, and Ireland, the eighteenth, and of Scotland the fifty-fourth. Anno Dom. 1620."

Plymouth Rock was not referenced by either William Bradford or Edward Winslow in their two primary documents about the landing. It was first mentioned in 1741 by Thomas Faunce, whose father had arrived in Plymouth in 1623.

"Which had been to their feet as a doorstep" comes from Henry Wadsworth Longfellow's poem, "Courtship of Miles Standish."

Quotes and text throughout the chapter are taken from William Bradford's **Of Plymouth Plantation,** *as rendered into Modern English by Harold Paget, 1909.*

Squanto was also known as Tisquantum.

The account of what we regard as the first Thanksgiving is found in Edward Winslow's **Mourt's Relations.**

A sachem is a paramount chief of North American tribes. Massasoit's name means "Great Sachem."

Pronunciation Guide:

Leyden – LIE-den

Samoset – SAM-uh-set

Patuxet – puh-TUX-et

Massosoit – MASS-uh-soyt

Wampanoag – WOMP-uh-nog or womp-uh-NOE-ag

Narragansetts – narr-uh-GAN-set

Chapter 23

The Founding of Massachusetts

For ten years after the coming of the Pilgrim Fathers, charters were constantly granted to "adventurers" of one kind or another for the founding of colonies in New England. And, driven by the tyranny of King James and of his son Charles I, small companies of Puritans began to follow the example of the Pilgrim Fathers and go out to New England, there to seek freedom to worship God. For King James, although brought up as a Presbyterian himself, was bitter against the Puritans. "I shall make them conform themselves," he had said, "or I will harry them out of the land."

And as he could not make them conform, he "harried" them so that many were glad to leave the land to escape tyranny. King James has been called the British Solomon, but he did some amazingly foolish things. This narrow-minded persecution of the Puritans was one. Yet by it he helped to form a great nation. So perhaps he was not so foolish after all.

As has been said, many companies were formed, many land charters granted for Northern Virginia, or New England, as it was now called. At length a company of Puritans under the name of the Massachusetts Bay Company got a charter from Charles I, granting them a large tract of land from three miles south of the Charles River to three miles north of the Merrimac, and as far west as the Pacific. Of course, no one in those days realized what a huge tract that would be. For no man yet guessed how great a continent America was, or by what thousands of miles the Pacific was separated from the Atlantic.

This charter was not unlike that given to Virginia. But there was one important difference. Nowhere in the charter did it say that the seat of government must be in England.

So when Charles dismissed his Parliament, vowing that if the members would not do as he wished he would rule without them, a great many Puritans decided to leave the country. They decided also to take their charter with them and remove the Company of Massachusetts Bay, bag and baggage, to New England.

Charles did nothing to stop them. Perhaps at the time he was pleased to see so many powerful Puritans leave the country, for without them he was all the freer to go his own way. So in the spring of 1630, more than a thousand set sail, taking with them their cattle and household goods.

Many of these were cultured gentlemen who were thus giving up money, ease, and position in order to gain freedom of religion. They were not poor laborers or artisans, not even for the most part traders and merchants. They chose as Governor for the first year a Suffolk gentleman named John Winthrop. A new Governor was chosen every year, but John Winthrop held the post many times, twice being elected three years in succession. Although we may think that he was narrow in some things, he was a man of calm judgment and even temper and was in many ways a good Governor. From the day he set forth from England to the end of his life, he kept a diary, and it is from this diary that we learn nearly all we know of the early days of the colony.

We also know that he delivered a sermon before he and his fellow settlers reached landfall, challenging them to be knit together. He said,

> *For we must consider that we shall be as a city upon a hill. The eyes of all people are upon us. So that if we shall deal falsely with our God in this work we have undertaken, and so cause Him to withdraw His present help from us, we shall be made a story and a by-word through the world.*

It was in June of 1630 that Winthrop and his company landed at Salem, and although there were already little settlements at Salem and elsewhere, this may be taken as the real founding of Massachusetts. Almost at once Winthrop decided that Salem would not be a good center for the colony, and he moved southward to the Charles River, where he finally settled on a little hilly peninsula. There a township was founded and given the name of Boston, after the town of Boston in Lincolnshire, from which many of the settlers had come.

Although these settlers had more money and more knowledge of trading, the colony did not altogether escape the miseries which every other colony had so far suffered. And, less stout-hearted than the founders of Plymouth, some fled back again to England. But they were only a few, and for the most part the new settlers remained and prospered.

These newcomers were not Separatists like the Pilgrim Fathers, but Puritans. When they left England, they had no intention of separating themselves from the Church of England. They had only desired a simpler service. But when they landed in America, they did in fact separate from the Church of England. England was so far away; the great ocean was between them and all the laws of Church and King. It seemed easy to cast them off, and they did.

So bishops were done away with, great parts of the Common Prayer Book were rejected, and the service as a whole made much more simple. And as they wished to keep their colony free of people who did not think as they did, the founders of Massachusetts made a law that only Church members might have a vote.

With the Plymouth Pilgrims, however, Separatists though they were, these Puritans were on friendly terms. The Governors of the two colonies visited each other to discuss matters of religion and trade, and each treated the other with great respect and ceremony.

We read how when Governor Winthrop went to visit Governor Bradford, the chief people of Plymouth came forth to meet him without the town and led him to the Governor's house. There he and his companions were entertained in goodly fashion, feasting every day, and holding pious disputations. Then when he departed again, the Governor of Plymouth with the pastor and elders accompanied him half a mile out of the town in the dark.

But although the Puritans of Massachusetts were friendly enough with dissenters beyond their borders, they soon showed that within their borders there was to be no other Church than that which they had set up.

Two brothers, for instance, who wanted to have the Prayer Book used in full were calmly told that New England was no place for them, and they were shipped home again. Later a minister named Roger Williams was banished from Massachusetts, for he preached that there ought to be no connection between Church and State, that a man was responsible to God alone for his opinions, and that no man had a right to take from or give to another a vote because of the Church to which he belonged.

It seemed to Williams a deadly sin to have had anything whatever to do with the Church of England, a sin for which everyone ought to do public penance. He also said that the land of America belonged to the Native people, and not to the King of England. Therefore the King of England could not possibly give it to the settlers, and they ought to bargain for it with the Indians. Otherwise they could have no right to it.

This idea seemed perfectly preposterous to those old settlers, for, said they, "he chargeth King James to have told a solemn public lie, because in his patent he blessed God that he was the first Christian prince that had discovered this land." They might think little enough of their King in their hearts, but it was not for a mere nobody to start such a ridiculous theory as this.

We, looking back, can see that Williams was a good and pious man, a man before his time, right in many of his ideas, though not very wise, perhaps, in his way of pressing them upon others who did not understand them. But to his fellow colonists he seemed nothing but a firebrand and a dangerous heretic. So they bade him be gone out of their borders. He went southward to what is now Rhode Island, made friends with the Narragansatts there, bought from them some land, and founded the town of Providence.

Notes:

The diary was The History of New England, from 1630 to 1649, *by John Winthrop.*

"I will make them conform themselves" was said by King James at the Hampton Court Conference, January 16, 1604.

The "city on a hill" quote is from Winthrop's sermon "A Model of Christian Charity." The "city on a hill" is a reference that came from the Sermon on the Mount, and after Winthrop used it, the phrase was often repeated in American politics, most notably by President Ronald Reagan.

"He chargeth King James" quote is from The History of New England from 1630 to 1649, *by John Winthrop.*

Chapter 24

The Story of Harry Vane

About this time there came to Massachusetts a handsome young adventurer named Sir Harry Vane. His face "was comely and fair," his thick brown hair curly and long, so that he looked more like a Cavalier than a Puritan. He was in fact the eldest son of a Cavalier, one of the King's chosen councilors. But in spite of his birth and upbringing, in spite even of his looks, Harry Vane was a Puritan. And he gave up all the splendor of life at court, he left father and mother and fortune, and came to New England for conscience' sake.

"Sir Henry Vane hath as good as lost his eldest son, who is gone to New England for conscience' sake," wrote a friend. "He likes not the discipline of the Church of England; none of our ministers would give him the sacrament standing; no persuasions of our Bishops nor authority of his parents could prevail with him: let him go."

As soon as Harry Vane arrived in Massachusetts, he began to take an interest in the affairs of the colony. And perhaps because of his great name as much as his fair face, gray-haired men who had far more experience listened to his youthful advice and bowed to his judgment. And before six months were passed he, although a mere lad of twenty-three, was chosen as Governor. A new Governor, you remember, was chosen every year.

At home Harry Vane had been accustomed to the pomp and splendor of courts and now he began to keep far greater state as Governor than anyone had done before him. Because he was son and heir to a Privy Councilor in England, the ships in the harbor fired a salute when he was elected, and when he went to church or court of justice, a bodyguard of four soldiers marched before him wearing steel corslet and cap and carrying halberds. He made, too, a sort of royal progress through his little domain, visiting all the settlements.

But although begun with such pomp, Vane's year of office was by no means a peaceful one. He was young and inexperienced, and he was not strong enough to deal with questions which even the oldest among the settlers found hard to settle. Yet with boyish presumption he set himself to the task. And although he failed, he left his mark on the life of the colony. His was one more voice raised in the cause of freedom. His was one more hand pointing the way to toleration. But he was too tempestuous, too careless of tact, too eager to hurry to the good end. So instead of keeping the colony with him, he created dissension. People took sides, some eagerly supporting the young Governor, but a far larger party as eagerly opposing him.

So after nine months of office, Harry Vane saw that where he had meant to create fair order, his hand created only disorder. And utterly disheartened, he begged the Council to relieve him of the governorship and allow him to go home to England.

But when one of his friends stood up and spoke in moving terms of the great loss he would be, Harry Vane burst into tears and declared he would stay, only he could not bear all the squabbling that had been going on, nor to hear it constantly said that he was the cause of it.

Then, when the Council declared that if that was the only reason he had for going they could not give him leave, he repented of what he had said and declared he must go for reasons of private business, and that anything else he had said was only said in temper. Whereupon the court consented in silence to his going.

All this was not very dignified for the Governor of a state, but hardly surprising from a passionate youth who had undertaken a task too difficult for him and felt himself a failure. However, Vane did not go. He stayed on to the end of his time, and even sought to be re-elected.

But feeling against him was by this time far too keen. He was rejected as Governor, and not even chosen as one of the Council. This hurt him deeply, he sulked in a somewhat undignified manner, and at length in August sailed home, never to return.

He had flashed like a brilliant meteor across the dull life of the colony. He made strife at the time, but afterwards there was no bitterness. When the colonists were in difficulties, they were ever ready to ask help from Harry Vane, and he as readily gave it. Even his enemies had to acknowledge his uprightness and generosity. His great-hearted adversary, Winthrop, wrote, "he showed himself a true friend to New England, and a man of noble and generous mind."

He took a great part in the troublous times which now came upon England, and more than twenty years later he died bravely on the scaffold for the cause to which he had given his life.

Notes:

"Comely and fair" quote is taken from The Life of Sir Henry Vane the Younger, Statesman and Mystic, 1613-1662, *by John Willcock, 1913.*

"Sir Henry Vane hath as good as lost" is taken from a letter from George Garrard to Edward, Viscount Conway and Killultagh, September 18, 1635, The Life of Young Sir Henry Vane, *by James Kendall Hosmer, 1888.*

A Privy Councillor is an advisor to the Sovereign of the United Kingdom.

A steel corslet is a vest of armor, worn on the upper body. Halberds were weapons, with an axe atop a long pole.

"He showed himself a true friend to New England" is from John Winthrop's The History of New England from 1630 to 1649, *with notes by John Savage, 1825.*

Some references to Harry Vane the Younger in literature include:

—William Wordsworth's poem:

"Great men have been among us; hands that penned

And tongues that uttered wisdom--better none:

The later Sidney, Marvel, Harrington,

Young Vane, and others who called Milton friend..."

—John Milton's Sonnet 17:

"Vane, young in years, but in sage counsell old..."

Chapter 25

The Story of Anne Hutchinson and the Founding of Rhode Island

About a year before Harry Vane came to Massachusetts, another interesting and brilliant colonist arrived. This was a woman named Anne Hutchinson. She was a midwife and a mother, very clever, "a woman of a ready wit and bold spirit." Like Williams she was in advance of her times, and like him she soon became a religious leader. She was able, she was deeply interested in religion, and she saw no reason why women should not speak their minds on such matters.

Men used to hold meetings to discuss questions of religion and politics, to which women were not allowed to go. Anne Hutchinson thought this was insulting, and she began to hold meetings for women in her own home. These meetings became so popular that often as many as a hundred women would be present. They discussed matters of religion, and as Mrs. Hutchinson held what the church leaders deemed "dangerous errors" about "grace and works" and justification and sanctification, news about this spread throughout the colony.

By the time that Harry Vane was chosen Governor, the matter had become serious. All the colony took sides for or against. Harry Vane, who stood for toleration and freedom, sided with Mrs. Hutchinson, while John Winthrop, his great rival, sided against her. Mrs. Hutchinson was supported and encouraged in her views by her brother-in-law John Wheelright, a "silenced minister sometimes in England."

The quarrel affected the whole colony and was viewed as a threat to its future. But so long as Harry Vane was Governor, Mrs. Hutchinson continued her preaching and teaching. When he sailed home, however, and Winthrop was Governor once more, the elders of the community decided that Mrs. Hutchinson was a danger to the colony and must be silenced. So all the elders and leaders met together in assembly and condemned her opinions, some as being "blasphemous, some erroneous, and all unsafe."

A few women, they decided, might without serious wrong meet together to pray and edify one another. But that a large number of sixty or more should do so every week was agreed to be "disorderly, and without rule." And as Mrs. Hutchinson would not cease her preaching and teaching, but firmly continued in her preaching, she was excommunicated and exiled from the colony.

Like Williams, Mrs. Hutchinson went to Rhode Island. To the sorrow of many, her husband went with her. And when they tried to bring him back, he refused. "For," he said, "I am more dearly tied to my wife than to the Church. And I do think her a dear saint and servant of God."

In Rhode Island, Mrs. Hutchinson and her friends founded the towns of Portsmouth and Newport. Others who had been driven out of one colony or another followed them, and other towns were founded. At length, however, all these little settlements joined together under one Governor.

At first the colony had no charter and occupied the land only by right of agreement with the Narragansatts. But after some time, Roger Williams got a charter from Charles II. In this charter it was set down that no one should be in "any wise molested, punished, disquieted, or called in question, for any differences in opinione in matters of religion." Thus another new state was founded, and in Rhode Island there was more real freedom than in almost any other colony in New England.

Massachusetts was at this time, as we can see, not exactly an easy place to live in for any one whose opinions differed in the slightest from those laid down by law. Those same people who had left their homes to seek freedom of conscience denied it to others. But they were so very, very sure that their way was the only right way, that they could not understand how anyone could think otherwise. They were good and honest men. And though they were severe with their fellows who strayed from the narrow path, it was their belief that by punishing them in this life, they might save them from much more terrible punishment in the life to come.

Notes:

Some quotes are from John Winthrop's Journal A History of New England, 1630-1649, volume 1. *The entire trial of Anne Hutchinson is written in John Winthrop's* "A short story of the rise, reign, and ruin of the Antinomians, Familists, and libertines that infected the churches of New-England..."

The "matters of religion" quote is from Charles II's Charter of Rhode Island and Providence Plantations - *July 15, 1663."*

Chapter 26

The Founding of Harvard

One very good thing we have to remember about the first settlers of Massachusetts is that early in the life of the colony, they founded schools and colleges. A good many of the settlers were Oxford and Cambridge men, though more indeed came from Cambridge than from Oxford, as Cambridge was much the more Puritan of the two. But whether from Oxford or from Cambridge, they were eager that their children born in this New England should have as good an education as their fathers had had in Old England. So when Harry Vane was Governor, the colonists voted 400 pounds with which to build a school. This is the first time known to history that the people themselves voted their own money to found a school, and this for the advanced training of ministers.

It was decided to build the school at New-Town. But the Cambridge men did not like the name, so they got it changed to Cambridge, "to tell their Posterity whence they came."

Shortly before this, a young Cambridge man named John Harvard had come out to Massachusetts. Very little is known of him save that he came from a prosperous family, and that he was good and learned. "A godly gentleman and lover of learning," old writers call him. "A scholar and pious in his life, and enlarged towards the country and the good of it, in life and in death."

Soon after he came to Boston, this godly gentleman was made minister of the church at Charlestown. But he was very delicate and in a few months he died.

As a scholar and a Cambridge man, he had been greatly interested in the building of the college at Cambridge. So when he died, he left half his money and all his books to it. The settlers were very grateful for this bequest, and to show their gratitude they decided to name the college after John Harvard.

Thus the first University in America was founded. From the beginning, the college was a pleasant place, "more like a bowling green than a wilderness," said one man. "The buildings were thought by some to be too gorgeous for a wilderness, and yet too mean in others' apprehensions for a college."

"The edifice," says another, "is very faire and comely within and without; (where they daily meet at commons, lectures, exercises), having in it a spacious hal, and a large library with some bookes to it."

Of Harvard's own books there were over three hundred, a very good beginning for a library in those far-off days. But unfortunately, they were all burnt about a hundred years later when the library accidentally took fire. Only one book was saved, as it was not in the library at the time.

Harvard's books are gone, nor does anything now remain of the first buildings "so faire and comely within and without." But the memory of the old founders and their wonderful purpose and energy is still kept green, and over the chief entrance of the present buildings are carved some words taken from a writer of those times. "After God had carried us safe to New-England, and wee had builded our houses, provided necessaries for our livelihood, rear'd convenient places for God's worship, and settled the Civill Government: One of the next things we longed for, and looked after was to advance Learning and perpetuate it to Posterity; dreading to leave an illiterate Ministry to the Churches, when our present ministers shall be in the Dust."

John Harvard was a good and simple man. In giving his money to found a college he had no thought of making himself famous. But "he builded better than he knew," for he reared for himself an eternal monument, and made his name famous to all the ends of the earth. And when kings and emperors are forgotten the name of Harvard will be remembered.

Notes:

"To tell their Posterity" and "more like a bowling green" are quotes from Captain Edward Johnson's The Wonderworking Providence of Sion's Saviour in New England, *the first printed history of New England.*

"The edifice" quote is from a booklet entitled New England's First Fruits, *1643.*

"After God had carried us safe" is inscribed on a plaque at Johnson Gate at Harvard University.

"He builded better than he knew" is from Ralph Waldo Emerson's poem, "The Problem."

Chapter 27

How Quakers First Came to New England

It was about the middle of the seventeenth century when a new kind of religion arose. This was the religion of the Quakers. George Fox was the founder of this sect, and they called themselves the Friends of Truth. The name Quaker was given to them by their enemies in derision because they "trembled at the word of the Lord."

The Quakers were a peace-loving people, they tried to be kind and charitable, they refused to go to law, and they refused to fight. They also gave up using titles of all kinds. For, "my Lord Peter and my Lord Paul are not to be found in the Bible." They refused to take off their hats to any man, believing that that was a sign of worship which belonged to God only. They refused also to take oath of any kind, even the oath of allegiance to the King, because Christ had said, "Swear not at all." They used "thee" and "thou" instead of "you" in speaking to a single person (because they thought it more simple and truthful in making everyone equal), and they refused to say "good night" or "good morrow," "for they knew the night was good, and the day was good, without wishing of either." There was a great deal that was good in their religion and very little, it would seem, that was harmful, but they were pronounced to be "mischievous and dangerous people."

Men did not understand the Quakers. And, as often happens when men do not understand, they became afraid of them. Because they wore black clothes and broad-brimmed hats, they thought they must be Jesuits in disguise. So ignorance bred fear, and fear brought forth persecution, and on all sides the Quakers were hunted and reviled.

They were fined and imprisoned, scourged and exiled, and sold into slavery. Then, like other persecuted people, they sought a refuge in New England across the seas. But the people there were just as ignorant as the people at home, and the Quakers found no kindly welcome.

The first Quakers to arrive in New England were two women, Mary Fisher and Ann Austin. But before they were allowed to land, officers were sent on board the ship to search their boxes. They found a great many books, which they carried ashore, and while the women were kept prisoner on board the ship, the books were burned in the marketplace by the common hangman. Then the women were brought ashore and sent to prison, for no other reason than that they were Quakers.

No one was allowed to speak to them on pain of a fine of five pounds, and lest any should attempt it, even the windows of the prison were boarded up. They were allowed no candle, and their pens, ink, and paper were taken from them. They might have starved but that one good old man named Nicholas Upsal, whose heart was grieved for them, paid the jailer to give them food. Thus they were kept until a ship was ready to sail for England. Then they were put on board, and the captain was made to swear that he would put them ashore nowhere but in England.

"Such," says an old writer, "was the entertainment the Quakers first met with at Boston, and that from a people, who pretended, that for conscience-sake they had chosen the wilderness of America before the well-cultivated old England."

The next Quakers who arrived were treated much in the same fashion and sent back to England, and a law was made forbidding Quakers to come to the colony. At this time, the same good old man who had already befriended them was grieved. Upsal warned them to "take heed that they were not found fighting against God, and so draw down a judgment upon the land." But the men of Boston were seized with a frenzy of hate and fear, and they banished this old man because he had dared to speak kindly of the accursed sect.

It is true the men of New England had some excuse for trying to keep the Quakers out of their colony. For some of them were foolish and tried to force their opinions noisily upon others. They interrupted the Church services, mocked the magistrates and the clergy, and some, carried away by religious fervor, behaved more like mad folk than the disciples of a religion of love and charity. And the people of New England, having escaped a country that did not allow freedom to choose one's religion, wanted to keep their new land for their own religion only.

Yet in spite of the law forbidding them to come, Quakers kept on coming to the colony, and all who came were imprisoned, beaten, and then thrust forth with orders never to return. But still they came. So a law was made that any Quaker coming into the colony should have one of his ears cut off. If he came again he should have a second ear cut off, and if he came a third time he should have his tongue bored through with a hot iron.

But even this cruel law had no effect upon the Quakers. They heeded it not, and they came in as great or even greater numbers than before.

The people of Boston were in despair. They had no wise to be cruel; indeed, many hated, and were thoroughly ashamed of, the cruel laws, made against these strange people. But they were nevertheless determined that Quakers should not come into their land. So now they made a law that any Quaker who came to the colony and refused to go away again when ordered should be hanged. This, they thought, would certainly keep these pernicious folk away. But it did not.

For the Quakers were determined to prove to all the world that they were free to go where they would, and that if they chose to come to Boston no man-made laws should keep them out. So they kept on coming. The magistrates knew not what to do. They had never meant to hang any of them, but only to frighten them away. But having made the law, they were determined to fulfill it, and four Quakers were hanged, one of them a woman. But while one was being tried another Quaker named Christison, who had already been banished, calmly walked into the court.

When they saw him, the magistrates were struck dumb. For they saw that against determination like this no punishment, however severe, might avail. On their ears, Christison's words fell heavily.

"I am come here to warn you," he cried, "that you should shed no more innocent blood: for the blood that you have shed already, cries to the Lord God for vengeance to come upon you."

Nevertheless, he, too, was seized and tried. But he defended himself well. "By what law will you put me to death?" he asked.

"We have a law," replied the magistrates, "and by our law you are to die."

"So said the Jews of Christ," replied Christison. "'We have a law, and by our law he ought to die.' Who empowered you to make that law? How have you power to make laws different from the laws of England. You are gone beyond your bounds. Are you subjects to the King? Yea or nay?"

"Yea, we are so."

"Well," said Christison, "so am I. Therefore seeing that you and I are subjects to the King, I demand to be tried by the laws of my own nation. For I never heard nor read of any law that was in England to hang Quakers."

Yet in spite of his brave defense, Christison was condemned to death. But the sentence was never carried out. For the people had grown weary of these cruelties; even the magistrates, who for a time had been carried away by blind hate, saw that they were wrong. Christison and many of his friends who had lain in prison awaiting trial were set free.

The Quakers, too, now found a strange friend in King Charles. For the doings of the New Englanders in this matter reached even his careless ears, and he wrote to his "trusty and well-beloved" subjects bidding them cease their persecutions and send the Quakers back to England to be tried. This the people of Massachusetts never did. But henceforth the persecutions died down. And although from time to time the Quakers were still beaten and imprisoned no more were put to death. At length the persecution died away altogether and the Quakers, allowed to live in peace, became quiet, hard-working citizens.

Notes:

In George Fox's autobiography, he says on p. 125, "This was Justice Bennet, of Derby, who was the first that called us Quakers, because I bade them tremble at the word of the Lord. This was in the year 1650." From George Fox's Journal, Volume 1.

"My Lord Peter and my Lord Paul" quote can be found in A Collection of the Works of William Penn in Two Volumes, *Volume 1, p. 324.*

"For they knew night was good" is from A Journal or Historical Account of the Life (Travels, etc.) of George Fox, *p. xvi.*

"Swear not at all" is from Matthew 5:34.

"Mischievous and dangerous people" is from Justin Winsor's English explorations and settlements in North America, 1497-1689, *p. 473.*

Other quotes are from A History of the Rise, Increase, and Progress of the Christian People Called Quakers, *Volume 1, by William Sewel, 1844.*

The four Boston martyrs executed between 1659 and 1661 were William Robinson, Marmaduke Stephenson, Mary Dyer, and William Leddra.

Henry Wadsworth Longfellow wrote about Wenlock Christison's trial in his play John Endicott, *which is part of* The New England Tragedies.

Chapter 28

How Maine and New Hampshire Were Founded

North of Massachusetts two more colonies, New Hampshire and Maine, were founded. But they were not founded by men who fled from tyranny, but by statesmen and traders who realized the worth of America, not by Puritans, but by Churchmen and Royalists. The two men who were chiefly concerned in the founding of these colonies were Sir Ferdinando Gorges and Captain John Mason. They were both eager colonists, and they both got several charters and patents from the King and from the New England Company.

It would be too confusing to follow all these grants and charters or all the attempts at settlements made by Mason and Gorges and others. The land granted to them was often very vaguely outlined, the fact being that the people who applied for the land and those who drew up the charters had only the vaguest ideas concerning the land in question. So the grants often overlapped each other, and the same land was frequently claimed by different people, and of course confusion and quarrels followed.

In 1629 Mason and Gorges, being friends, agreed to divide the province of Maine between them, and Mason called his part New Hampshire, after the county of Hampshire in England, of which he was fond. Mason and Gorges each now had an enormous tract of land, but they wanted still more.

The French, as you know, had already made settlements in Canada. But just at this time that buccaneering sea captain, David Kirke,

211

besieged Quebec, took it and carried its brave governor, Samuel de Champlain, away prisoner. Now, as soon as they heard of this Gorges and Mason asked the King to give them a grant of part of the conquered land, for it was known to be a fine country for fur trade and was also believed to be rich in gold and silver mines. In answer to this petition the King granted a great tract of land to Gorges and Mason. This they called Laconia because it was supposed to contain many lakes. They never did much with it, however, and in a few years when peace was made with France, it had all to be given back to the French.

Both Mason and Gorges spent a great deal of money trying to encourage colonists to settle on their land, and the people of Massachusetts were not at all pleased to have such powerful Churchmen for their neighbors.

As has been said, land grants often overlapped, and part of the land granted to Gorges and Mason was also claimed by Massachusetts. The Massachusetts colonists insisted on their rights. Both Gorges and Mason therefore became their enemies and did their best to have their charter taken away. To this end Gorges got himself made Governor General of the whole of New England with power to do almost as he liked, and he made ready to set out for his new domain with a thousand soldiers to enforce his authority.

When this news reached Massachusetts, the whole colony was thrown into a frenzy. For in this appointment the settlers saw the end of freedom, the beginning of tyranny. Both Gorges and his friend Mason were zealous Churchmen, and the Puritans felt sure they would try to force them all to become Churchmen also.

This the settlers determined to resist with all their might. So they built forts round Boston Harbor and mounted cannon ready to sink any hostile vessel which might put into port. In every village the young men trained as soldiers, and a beacon was set up on the highest point of the triple hill upon which Boston is built. And daily these young men turned their eyes to the hill, for when a light appeared there, they knew it would be time to put on their steel caps and corslets and march to defend their liberties. Ever since, the hill has been called Beacon Hill.

But the danger passed. The new ship which was being built for Ferdinando Gorges mysteriously fell to pieces on the very launching of it, and Captain Mason died. "He was the chief mover in all the attempts against us," says Winthrop. "But the Lord, in mercy, taking him away, all the business fell on sleep."

But still Gorges did not give up his plans. He did not now go out to New England himself as he had meant to do but sent first his nephew and then his cousin instead. They, however, did not trouble Massachusetts much.

Over the Province of Maine, Sir Ferdinando ruled supreme. He could raise troops, make war, give people titles, levy taxes. No one might settle down or trade in his province without his permission, and all must look upon him as the lord of the soil and pay him tribute. It was the feudal system come again, and Sir Ferdinando Gorges was as near being a king as any ruler of America ever has been. He drew up a most elaborate constitution, too, for his kingdom, making almost more offices than there were citizens to fill them. For, after all, his kingdom was a mere wilderness containing two fishing villages and here and there a few scattered settlements. And when the deputy governor arrived to rule this kingdom, he found his "palace" merely a broken-down store house with "nothing of his household-stuff remaining but an old pot, a pair of tongs, and a couple of cob-irons."

Thus side by side with the Puritan colonies of New England, colonies which were almost republics, there was planted a feudal state which was almost a monarchy. Of all the New England colonies, New Hampshire and Maine were the only two which were not founded for the sake of religion. For although the English Church was established in both as the state religion, that was merely because the proprietors were of that Church. The colonies were founded for the sake of trade and profit. But they grew very slowly.

In 1647 Sir Ferdinando Gorges died, and Maine was left much to itself. For his son John took little interest in his father's great estate. Thirty years later his grandson, another Ferdinando, sold his rights to Massachusetts. From that time till 1820, when it was admitted to the Union as a separate state, Maine was a part of Massachusetts.

Neither did the heirs of Mason pay much attention to their estates at first. And when they did there was a good deal of quarreling and a good deal of trouble, and at length they sold their rights to twelve men, who were afterwards known as the Masonian Proprietors.

There was a great deal of trouble, too, before New Hampshire was finally recognized as a separate colony. It was joined to Massachusetts and separated again more than once. But at last, after many changes, New Hampshire finally became a recognized separate colony. And although Captain John Mason died long before this happened, he has been called the founder of New Hampshire.

"If the highest mortal honor," it has been said, "belongs to founders of states, as Bacon has declared, then Mason deserved it. To seize on a tract of the American wilderness, to define its limits, to give it a name, to plant it with an English colony, and to die giving it his last thoughts among worldly concerns, are acts as lofty and noble as any recorded in the history of colonization."

Notes:

Churchmen were those who followed the Church of England.

While Samuel de Champlain was not actually the Governor of Quebec, the people gave him this title. Biographer David Hackett Fischer wrote, "Even when the title of governor was officially denied by Richelieu, the people of Quebec gave it to him anyway. They called him their governor, often 'our governor,' even 'my governor.'" **Champlain's Dream***, Simon & Schuster, New York, NY, 2008, p.446.*

"He was the chief mover" quote is taken from **The History of New England from 1630 to 1649** *by John Winthrop, p. 223.*

"Nothing of his household-stuff remaining" quote is from **The History of the State of Maine***, by William Durkee Williamson, 1839, p. 283.*

"If the highest honor" quote is taken from **A briefe discourse of the Nevv-found-land with the situation, temperature, and commodities thereof, inciting our nation to goe forward in that hopefull plantation begunne***, or* **Captain John Mason, the Founder of New Hampshire***, Boston: Prince Society, 1887, p. 30. The quote is from the portion that is a memoir by Charles Wesley Tuttle. (The reference to Francis Bacon is from*

Francis Bacon's Essays, Essay LVII, "Honour and Reputation.")

Included in John Mason's life in America is the Pequot War and the Mystic Massacre, which are written about in the next chapter and so will be contained in Volume 2 of **This Country of Ours.**

Pronuncation Guide:

Gorges – GOR-jez

Champlain – sham-PLANE

Laconia – luh-KONE-ee-uh

Made in the USA
Las Vegas, NV
05 September 2023

77074304R00134